The Lost Population

The Lost Population

Status Offenders in America

Robert Hartmann McNamara
THE CITADEL

CAROLINA ACADEMIC PRESS

Durham, North Carolina

Copyright © 2008
Robert Hartmann McNamara
All rights reserved.

Library of Congress Cataloging-in-Publication Data

McNamara, Robert Hartmann.
  The lost population : status offenders in America / by Robert
Hartmann McNamara.
    p. cm.
  Includes bibliographical references and index.
  ISBN-13: 978-1-59460-359-4 (alk. paper)
  ISBN-10: 1-59460-359-6 (alk. paper)
  1. Juvenile delinquents--United States. 2. Runaway teenagers--
United States. 3. Homeless teenagers--United States. 4.
Teenagers--Substance use--United States. I. Title.

  HV9104.M36 2008
  364.360973--dc22

                                                    2007044853

Carolina Academic Press
700 Kent Street
Durham, North Carolina 27701
Telephone: (919) 489-7486
Fax: (919) 493-5668
www.cap-press.com

Printed in the United States of America

To the Case and Taylor children:
Shannon, Audrey, Kevin, Ryan, Sarah and Daniel:
I pray that you never become involved
in any of the activities described in this book.

Contents

Tables and Illustrations

Preface

My interest in status offenders began many years ago when I taught a delinquency class at a local university while attending graduate school. At that time there was little in the way of empirical information other than historical accounts of the deinstitutionalization of status offenders during the 1970s. I wanted to return to this topic some day and offer a book like this one so that students who were taking a course on delinquency or child welfare could see the connections of these seemingly innocuous behaviors to larger and more serious forms of delinquency. Little did I realize that such a connection would become the driving force behind public policy. While it is true that many status offenders also engage in other forms of traditional delinquency, I think we have made a mistake in assuming that if a youth runs away from home, it is an indication that they are a chronic delinquent. This is true even if the youth repeatedly runs away. Instead I think there are differing degrees of status offenders and to put them all into the same category of "delinquent" not only raises serious questions about our understanding of juvenile crime in general, it will likely result in a self-fulfilling prophecy, where the youth actually begins to engage in serious youth crime. In other words, in the process of implementing a tough law and order approach to delinquency we may be augmenting the very class of individuals we most fear. My hope is that this book will shed some light on the nuances and problems relating to behaviors such as running away, truancy, and curfew violations. Additionally, I hope it sheds light on other behaviors that indirectly affect criminal behavior and have a significant impact on society. Underage drinking and smoking present two of the most serious social problems connected to teens in America, yet despite warnings and alarming trends, we seem to be minimizing or ignoring their impact. In short, I believe the public's fears about violent juvenile crime have overshadowed virtually all aspects of juvenile justice and we appear to be returning to a time when we treated juveniles and adults alike in terms of punishment. There may be good reasons for doing this, however, but a sizeable portion of youth exist who are actually victims of neglectful and abusive parents, dysfunctional families, or are caught in difficult circumstances that result in their coming to the attention of the justice process. I believe this book can serve as a starting point for a new dialogue about status offenders and to find ways to keep them from becoming hardened delinquents.

RHM

Acknowledgments

A project such as this one cannot be undertaken without a significant amount of assistance. Many thanks go to The Citadel Foundation for their financial support during the course of this project. Similarly, I would like to thank my Department Chair, Gardel Feurtado, for his support and understanding in allowing me time to work on this book. Being a faculty member at a primarily teaching institution means there is often little time for scholarship. Thankfully, my colleagues at The Citadel understand this and have allowed me the time, resources, and space to explore a topic in depth. Additionally, I am grateful for the assistance of Dr. Maria Shelley and Ms. Lucy Clark Sanders for their invaluable help in bringing this project to completion. Similarly, Bob Conrow at Carolina Academic Press has been one of the most supportive editors I have had the privilege to work with over the span of my career. Finally, I would like to thank my wife Carey for being so patient and understanding during the course of this project and in the latter stages of writing this book.

The Lost Population

The Lost Population:
Status Offenders in America

- A teenager is found living in an abandoned building with several other youth.
- A high school student skips school and hangs out with friends in the mall.
- A group of teenage boys convince an adult to purchase liquor for them on a Friday night.
- A couple brings their child to Family Court after he consistently refuses to obey the rules of the household.
- A fourteen year old boy produces a fake ID and buys a pack of cigarettes.
- A youth hangs out with his friends in a park after 11pm on a school night.

Any of these behaviors could be observed in cities across the country and are relatively mild in terms of their severity. Some experts might contend that these are problems for individual families to work out, or what C. Wright Mills termed "personal troubles," and are not the government's responsibility to solve. Others claim that such behaviors reflect a much more serious problem that has far reaching implications. While these behaviors would not be considered criminal if committed by adults, they are known as *status offenses* and can result in the child becoming involved in the juvenile justice system. Status offenses include running away, truancy, ungovernability (or what is sometimes called incorrigibility), curfew violations, underage drinking, and underage smoking (Office of Juvenile Justice Delinquency Prevention 2006).

Status offenses have a long and controversial history in the juvenile justice system. Even today there remains a debate about whether or not formal social control is the appropriate response for such offenders. After all, these are not serious crimes nor are they necessarily a threat to the general public—in fact, many are relatively common adolescent behaviors. However, some do reflect more serious issues, such as the consequences of underage drinking and the harmful effects of smoking. The treatment of status offenses is complicated, particularly in light of the fact that a movement towards punishment, particularly for juveniles, has taken place in the United States. There are many examples of youthful offenders who commit violent crimes and such episodes create a heightened sense of fear among the public. The result is pressure on policymakers to increase punitive measures for all offenders. While it is understandable that violent offenders should be punished, the same tactic applied to minor offenses can have many negative implications.

Adolescence in the New Millenium

What is it like to be a teenager in the 21st century? What behaviors are considered acceptable and which ones are out of bounds? Are kids today really that different from those in the past or is everything relative to time, place and circumstance? The answers, in part, are found in the characteristics and values of each generation.

After World War II ended, the United States experienced an explosion of births, nearly 76 million from 1946 to 1964. Sociologists define those born during those years as *Baby Boomers*. This group currently represents about 28% of the U.S. population and is responsible for some of the most dramatic changes in American history. From the Vietnam War protests to the Civil Rights Movement to the rise of feminism and the hippie movement, Baby Boomers have been at the center of the debate, discussion, and social change. This group, many of whom turned 60 years old in 2006, comprises some of the country's leading politicians, entertainers, and social activists. Baby Boomers have also been referred to as the "Me" generation for their emphasis on narcissism and individual pleasure. In fact, this group has fundamentally altered the way in which the elderly are understood in American society. Not content to simply age gracefully like their parents, this group has remained healthy, wealthy, and active into their retirement years. As a result, Baby Boomers have changed the way most Americans perceive of normal aging (U.S. Census Bureau 2006).

Baby Boomers focused on their careers, leisure activities, and many delayed having children or remained childless. As a result, an anticipated second Baby Boom generation did not occur. The subsequent generation, clearly smaller in size, consisting of about 41 million, were born roughly between 1968 and 1979. These are often referred to as *Generation X (Gen Xers)*. Many experts argue that this group has often been ignored and misunderstood. Gen Xers are generally marked by their lack of optimism for the future and an absence of trust in traditional values. During the early 1990s, the media portrayed Gen Xers as a group of overeducated, underachieving "slackers," who are more concerned with tattoos, body piercing, and who spawned the grunge music movement.

Gen Xers grew up during the end of the Cold War, the Reagan administration, and witnessed the economic depression of the 1990s. Many members of this generation watched as their parents coped with the loss of their careers and jobs due to outsourcing, deindustrialization, and corporate mergers. This had a profound impact on many Gen Xers, who realized that company loyalty and sacrifices to get ahead did not always pay off. As a result, many Gen Xers did not take advantage of their education or talents and ended up in *McJobs*, or jobs in the lowest paying sectors of the market, including many that paid minimum wages. This lack of stability in the job market left many Gen Xers with a strong sense of cynicism about their lives, future, and the country as a whole. This group is also generally critical of the Baby Boomer generation, whom many Gen Xers look upon as self-centered and impractical (IT Management 2006).

Generation Y (Gen Yers), those born approximately between 1977 and 1994, make up over 20% of the U.S. population or 70 million people. This generation is a large one and they are likely to have a significant impact on this country's social and economic landscape in the future. Generation Y is characterized by three main elements. First, members are comfortable and tolerant of the racial and ethnic diversity around them and feel comfortable interacting with people outside their own ethnic group.

Second, one of the most noted trends in the Generation Y segment of the population is that the parents of Gen Yers are very involved in the daily lives and decisions of their children. Parents often help Gen Yers plan their achievements, take part in their daily activities and strongly encourage their children to succeed. This encouragement makes members of the Y Generation believe they can accomplish anything. Their relationship with parents also makes it more likely for Gen Yers to feel they can always return home for support and assistance.

Third, an important characteristic of this generation is that its members are technologically savvy—Gen Yers tend to be more sophisticated in their computer skills than previous groups. This is largely due to being exposed to and using technology at an early age. For instance, three out of four teenagers are on-line and 93% of those ages 15–17 are computer users. The time spent on-line consists of gaming, emailing, and instant messaging according to the National Center for Health Statistics. In short, this group is educated, technologically adept and have been encouraged by their parents that they can achieve whatever goals they set for themselves. It is not surprising to learn, then, that there is a strong sense of entitlement felt by this group about wanting the best in life and thinking they deserve it (NAS Recruitment Communication 2006).

This generation is ambitious and has high expectations of themselves and those around them. It also means this group is accustomed to instant gratification and tends to be overly confident. This group is also often characterized as those who are willing to cheat, if necessary, to achieve their goals. On the positive side, this group is very adaptable in a variety of settings, are efficient multi-taskers, and possess the technological skills and educational talents to achieve significant goals.

Thus, the social world of the teenager is very different from earlier generations. Tivo, Instant Messaging, iPods, Wifi, technology, population growth, and a postmodernist world have created a number of unique challenges to today's teen. The U.S. Census Bureau estimated in 2002 that there were 72,895,500 persons under the age of

18 in this country, or about 25% of all U.S. residents. Additionally, current projections indicate that this segment of the population will increase by 14% between 2000 and 2025 and by 2050, the population will be over a third larger than it was in 2000. The newest generation of teens have been raised with high expectations, a sense of entitlement, and a confidence not seen in other generations. As a result, some of the behaviors 21st century teens engage in might reflect more of the value system and family structure than the individual decisions of particular offenders. This is true of status offenders as well as serious or violent delinquents.

The History of Status Offenders

A historical basis exists for status offense statutes. It was common practice in early America to place disobedient or runaway youths in orphan asylums, residential homes, or houses of refuge. In 1646 the Massachusetts Stubborn Child Law was enacted, which provided that "if any man have a stubborn and rebellious status offender of sufficient years and understanding, which will not obey the voice of his father or his mother, and that when they have chastened him will not harken unto them, they could bring him before the court and testify that he would not obey. If the magistrate then found the child to be unrepentant and incapable of control, such a child could be put to death." (Tyler, Segady, and Austin 2000).

Until the 1970s, there was no significant legal distinction between a juvenile who committed a criminal act, a juvenile who was considered a wayward youth, and a child who came from a home with unwilling, destitute, or deceased parents. Under the doctrine of *parens patriae*, the Juvenile Court believed that it had the duty to intervene if doing so was in the child's best interests. The court could address any behavior or circumstance causing concern, whether the behavior was delinquent or not. As a result, the caseloads in many jurisdictions consisted mainly of non-delinquents (Steinhart 1996).

Because all youths coming to juvenile court were considered to have demonstrated a behavior or circumstance indicating the need for court intervention, it followed that the legal process did not differ much for the hardened delinquent and the vagrant youth. The outcome was that many non-delinquent youth were institutionalized in the same facilities with serious offenders prior to the 1970s. This melding of the two types of offenders resulted in a number of issues. For example, the indeterminate sentencing structure in juvenile courts meant that offenders would remain incarcerated until they were "fixed" or cured of their behavior (Seigel, Welsh, and Senna 2005). Clearly this philosophy created problems for status offenders because they were often incarcerated not on the basis of their own behavior, but because their parents failed to adequately provide for them. Consequently, many youth would remain under state care longer than their more serious counterparts largely because there was no place to release them.

Second, and perhaps more tragic, as many non-delinquents were incarcerated with serious offenders, not only did the risks of victimization increase (because they should have been separated from the more violent youth), many non-delinquents were exposed criminal colleagues and learned the techniques and rationalizations associated with this type of lifestyle (Seigel, Welsh, and Senna 2005).

As experts began to grasp the significance of these trends, policy changes began to emerge. In the 1960s a number of events led to the reexamination of how society treated status offenders. For example, in 1961, in one of the first acts by the Kennedy administration, the President's Committee on Juvenile Delinquency and Youth Crime focused federal attention on the problems of delinquency. Four years later the President's Commission on Law Enforcement and the Administration of Justice examined crime in America. The subsequent report on delinquency marked the first real distinction between a delinquent and a status offender. That same year control of delinquency was assigned to the Department of Justice under the Omnibus Crime Control and Safe Streets Act. The significance of this change is found in the differences between separate detention facilities for juveniles and adult offenders (Maxon and Klein 1997).

Perhaps the most significant piece of legislation as it relates to status offenders occurred in 1974 with the Juvenile Justice Delinquency Prevention Act (JJDPA). By then, the Department of Justice was given full authority over all delinquency matters, including status offenses. The act essentially separated the treatment of delinquents and status offenders as well as designating the responsibility for treatment. Essentially, it earmarked the care of status offenders to community agencies since status offenses were seen as treatable and offenders should not be stigmatized with a delinquency label (Maxon and Klein 1997).

While the change process began by making a legal distinction between youths who committed criminal acts and status offenders, the real value was the shift in focus from labeling them delinquents to *Children In Need of Supervision (CHINS), Minors in Need of Supervision (MINS),* or *Persons In Need of Supervision (PINS)* (Seigel, Welsh, and Senna 2005).

This language reflected the shift in philosophy and was underscored by the passage of the JJDPA in 1974. This legislation required the removal of non-delinquents from secure institutions such as detention centers and state schools and prohibited the practice of confining juveniles with adults. The core of the JJDPA was the deinstitutionalization of status offenses. That meant that youth who were classified as CHINS, MINS, and PINS could not be considered delinquent or treated that way. Second, should the occasion arise in which status offenders or non-delinquents need to be detained, they must be completely separated from adult offenders and prevented from any type of contact with them (Hutzler 1982).

It is important to note that this act did not mandate an immediate compliance by states. In fact, the act placed the Office of Juvenile Justice and Delinquency Prevention (OJJDP) in an awkward position. The legislation was designed to require states to protect status offenders and while they were required to comply with the act, if states refused, the only recourse the federal government had was to deny them the opportunity to apply for federal grants. Additionally, such a philosophical shift would require time to be put into effect. The OJJDP realized that the problem could not be solved overnight and that it would take states a number of years to make the corrections to existing delinquency policy (Maxon and Klein 1997).

Initially, the federal government allowed states to use federal funds for deinstitutionalization of status offender (DSO) projects of their own design for a pilot period of two to three years (Maxon and Klein

1997). Consequently, hundreds of proposals for programs to dein-stitutionalize status offenders were submitted but only twelve satis-fied OJJDP officials. Of these, only eight were accepted into the over-all DSO evaluation. The main reason so few were accepted was a requirement that agencies had to submit to an independent evalua-tion of their program.

Clearly officials at OJJDP felt that while confinement was unac-ceptable, other mechanisms had to be put in place to assist status of-fenders. Thus, rather than simply releasing status offenders into the community, where little help is offered and the community remains at some level of risk, the DSO evaluation required that some sort of alternative be offered that combined diversion, community treatment, and prevention within the community. Despite the stringent guide-lines and selection process, while the format and structure of these eight programs were varied, the effort was generally considered a fail-ure for each site (Kobrin and Klein 1997).

However, as Klein and Maxon (1997) found, analysis of aggregated cases showed that DSO clients on average committed crimes at a higher rate than the comparison youth who had been subject to detention. Ad-ditionally, the evaluation showed that DSO clients were more likely to be females who came from intact homes with less serious offense his-tories. The significance of this is that they would have been predicted to re-offend at a lower rate than the comparison group, not a higher one.

These results were not made public and as the Reagan adminis-tration took office in 1980, a second phase of deinstitutionalization began. What was most interesting about the findings of the study was that policymakers and practitioners believed that status offenders were a distinct category of youth who differed from delinquents. However, the DSO evaluation revealed that the majority of youths' prior offenses and recidivist patterns were as likely to be petty thefts and vandalism as they were to be charged with running away, incor-rigibility, or truancy. The implication of this is that youth who com-mit more than one offense do so in a wider pattern than simple sta-tus offenses. Given this, therapeutic responses to status offenses would be inappropriate and largely ineffective.

Runaways, in particular, presented the most difficult challenge to this conclusion. Most runners were not recidivists: most only had one episode. Second, it is hard to typify the "pure" runaway who only engages in this activity and no other form of delinquency. However, these were the most likely offenders to come to the attention of DSO agencies. While they were not truly serious cases, particularly since pure runaways were a small population, the most consistently applied service provided to them (psychological counseling) was more likely to be harmful than helpful and the most effective strategy would be to find residential placement. However, this was cost prohibitive. In sum, many status offenders were not that different from delinquents in terms of their behavior and runaways presented unique challenges in terms of treatment.

Amendments to JJDPA

The judicial response to the JJDPA was said by some experts to be a hostile one. In fact, some juvenile court judges viewed the JJDPA as a threat to their authority to enforce court orders. In 1980, judges successfully lobbied Congress to amend the JJDPA by creating an exception to the ban on detaining status offenders in secure facilities. Known as *the valid court order amendment*, this provision allowed secure detention of adjudicated status offenders who violated a valid order of the juvenile court (Steinhart 1996).

While generally juveniles would not be detained in adult jail and lockups, an exception was made in the event that the juvenile was being tried as an adult for a felony or had a felony conviction. Another exception to the detention prohibition was that juveniles could be held in an adult jail or lockup for six hours in urban areas and up to 24 hours in rural areas if no alternative arrangements could be made and secure detention was required (Seigel, Walsh, and Senna 2005).

Not all judges opposed deinstitutionalization, however. In a 1990 report, the Metropolitan Court Committee of the National Council of Juvenile and Family Court Judges argued that status offenders were most often victims, not offenders, and should not be treated as delinquents. In fact, the report called for court intervention as a last resort when all other community resources failed. The reality, sadly, is that since states have not made programs for status offenders a priority, court intervention occurs more often than one might suspect.[1]

The 1980s also witnessed less concern about the deinstitutionalization of status offenders and more upon serious and violent juvenile offenders. This was based in part upon the general public's concern that serious juvenile crime had increased, the DSO programs that had been in use had not reduced recidivism, and there was reason to consider abandoning the original DSO objectives because of the findings that most status offenders committed delinquent acts (Klein and Maxon 1997). As Zatz (1982) has noted, there had not been agreement from the outset of what deinstitutionalization of status offenders meant. The variety of approaches by states had a wide range of effects on clients, agencies and the justice system. Thus, coupled with the general belief that status offenders were not that different from traditional delinquents, attention to DSO as well as the treatment of status offenders generally lost momentum.

The Problems of Treating Status Offenders as Delinquents

Some activists, advocates, and experts on delinquency contend that the deinstitutionalization of status offenders resulted in various means by which judges and juvenile courts have been able to circumvent federal law dictating how status offenders are treated. In essence they argue that these youth have been transformed from institution children, who are victims of dysfunctional families, to agency kids who are increasingly being incarcerated in the community. This is accomplished in two ways: bootstrapping and reclassifying status offenders as mentally ill.

---

1. Another amendment to the JJDPA occurred in 1992. This shift required states to address the disproportionality of minorities that were detained. Juvenile justice agencies must now determine the extent of the disproportionality, determine why it exists, and try to reduce it without employing quotas (Seigel, Walsh, and Senna 2005).

Bootstrapping

This is a process whereby a juvenile court elevates (or bootstraps) a status offender to a delinquent for repeated violations of the same offense. This can occur in two general ways: contempt of court and escape petitions. In the contempt of court explanation, assume that a child skips school and is identified as truant. He is brought before the court and the judge orders the child to attend school and requires parents to compel that child to go to school each day.

In this case, a formal order of the court is issued, mandating the child to go to school. Let's also say that the child refuses to comply with the court's request and continues to be truant. He is again caught and brought before the court. In response, the youth is then found to be in contempt of court for engaging in the same behavior. The court then elevates the contempt of court violation into a delinquent offense for violating a valid court order. This allows the youth to be held in a more secure and punitive setting, such as a detention center. The danger in bootstrapping is found in the fact that it creates the possibility that the youth will face an adjudication hearing for a delinquent act. This is significant since it now makes the youth eligible for institutionalization or a host of sanctions reserved for only delinquents (Seigel, Walsh, and Senna 2005).

The second way status offenders can be incarcerated is the violation of an escape petition. Let's say, for example, a juvenile judge sends a status offender to a group home for six months for running away. The child then runs away from this facility as well. Like the first example, in the eyes of the court, the child is now elevated in status to a delinquent. Although the youth's behavior did not change, it is still a violation of a valid court order which subjects the child to a delinquent status.

Even though federal law and some states prohibit bootstrapping and the use of secure facilities, many courts disregard these laws. Judges sometimes argue that the law diminishes the courts' contempt power to sanction status offenders and represents an unconstitutional infringement of judicial power. As a result, most courts have held that status offenders can be elevated to delinquent status for violation court orders even if the elevation to delinquent status is for the same status offense (Seigel, Walsh, and Senna 2005).

Hidden Delinquency

Another way to detain status offenders is through the use of alternative institutionalizations, usually mental hospitals and substance abuse treatment centers. Confinement to one of these facilities does not violate the mandates of JJDPA because such institutions are considered "treatment oriented" and not punitive in nature (Seigel, Walsh, and Senna 2005). Youths sent to these places are sometimes labeled *hidden delinquents* and are captured by a system that hides them under the guise of helping them.

It is interesting to note that youths committed to mental hospitals and other treatment-oriented institutions are usually afforded less due process than what delinquents normally receive in juvenile court. This is true despite the fact that they have not committed a crime and are still confined in a similar manner as traditional delinquents. In the landmark case of *Parham v. J.R.* 442 U.S. 584 (1979) 442 U.S. 584, the U.S. Supreme Court held that parents may commit their child to a mental hospital as long as there is some type of hearing conducted by an impartial party and evidence of a mental disorder is found. In those instances, the child may be held indefinitely until either the parents request that their child be released or when there is evidence that the child no longer suffers from a mental illness.

This practice has generated controversy. Some say that mental institutions and other placements have become an alternative way to incarcerate status offenders with their offending behavior used to show "evidence of mental illness" or a need for treatment. It is also important to note that the hidden system is not limited to substance abuse facilities or mental hospitals. As long as a status offender is not placed in a secure detention facility or state school, juvenile court judges have used a variety of residential or out-of-home placements. These places provide an alternative to institutional disposition to detention centers and state schools and are not subject to JJDPA deinstitutionalization guidelines (Seigel, Walsh, and Senna 2005).

Problems Studying Status Offenders Today

There are a variety of problems in determining the total number of status offenders in the United States. In some states, for example, status offenders cannot technically be arrested and even though they are taken into custody, they are not reflected in arrest statistics. As was mentioned in other states, status offenders are considered "in need of assistance" rather than criminals. This means their cases are more likely to be handled by social service agencies than the juvenile justice system. A related problem is that some status offense cases are not considered part of the official count unless a petition is filed in the case and the youth goes to court for an adjudication hearing (Stahl, et al. 2005). For all of these reasons, as in the case of adult crime, there remains a "dark figure" of status offenses.

Another reason the data on status offenses is questionable relates to the way the term is operationalized. For many, the term *status offense* is an umbrella designation covering numerous behaviors. For instance, some states define a status offender as a youth who is "incorrigible" or "stubborn," while many other states do not include this behavior in their official statistics. The reason is due to broad and uneven definitions—being stubborn is subject to a lot of interpretation, whereas there is less disagreement about behaviors such as underage drinking.

Despite problems in defining and tracking, certain categories of status offenses can be followed over time and circumstance. For example, the Uniform Crime Reports contains data concerning three main status offenses: running away, curfews violations, and underage drinking (liquor law) violations.

Information on these offenses are considered by experts to be more problematic behavior. Still, while official counts offer a somewhat clearer picture of serious offending in the United States, as with all official documentation of criminal behaviors, these reports suffer from a number of methodological limitations. This, in turn, fails to provide a complete and comprehensive picture of status offending (Stahl et al. 2005).

According to the Uniform Crime Reports, juveniles were arrested for an estimated 1.6 million offenses in 2005, roughly 320,000 of which were status offenses. Of those, 108,954 were for running away, 140,000 were for curfew violations and loitering, and 76,756 were liquor law violations. This is a significant decrease from 2001, where 2.3 million arrests were made, of which 400,000 were status offenders. The reason for the dramatic decrease is likely due to the fact that status offenses are being replaced with arrests for delinquent acts. That is, whether it is due to a shift in offending patterns or a reprioritizing by justice officials, arrests for status offenses have decreased. This demonstrates a significant departure from what was seen a decade earlier.

Perhaps the most comprehensive information available on status offenders comes from the *Juvenile Court Statistics* (JCS). This report uses data provided by the National Juvenile Court Data Archive by state and county agencies responsible for collecting and/or dissemination of information on the processing of youth in juvenile courts. It is important to note that these data are not derived from a complete census of juvenile courts or obtained from a probability sample of courts. Also, the number of cases presented by the JCS does not include status cases that were dealt with informally by social service agencies or juvenile courts without a petition. Thus, JCS reports only focus on petitioned cases. What the JCS represents then, are national estimates. Having said that, they have become one of the most widely accepted measures of delinquency in the United States and offer a profile of status offending.

Age

According to Juvenile Court Statistics in 2002, the most recent data available, law enforcement agencies referred about 40% of runaway cases and about 10% in truancy and ungovernability cases to juvenile court for disposition. As Table 1-1 shows, almost the same number of runaways come from either the age group 15 years old or younger or the age 16 or older age group. The same is true of ungovernability cases and liquor law violations.

Gender and Race

A major difference between delinquency and status offense cases is the large proportion of females in status offending. For instance, as

Table 1-1. Percentage of Petitioned Status Offense Cases by Age 1985–2002

	Age 15 or Younger	Age 16 or Older
All Status Offenses	9%	9%
Runaway	17%	16%
Ungovernability	10%	10%
Liquor	8%	7%
Truancy	4%	3%

Source: Juvenile Court Statistics 1985–2002

Table 1-2 shows, females represented 58% of runaways, 44% of truancy, and 46% of ungovernability cases, and nearly a quarter of liquor law violations. According to the Juvenile Court Statistics, from 1985–2002, the male and female proportions of truancy and ungovernability cases were roughly similar to their representation in the general population. Additionally, while runaway cases were disproportionately female, males were overrepresented in liquor law violations.

As Table 1-3 shows, overall White juveniles accounted for the majority of petitioned status offense cases, particularly liquor law violations, which comprised 87% of those detained.

Between 1985 and 2002, African Americans consisted of about a quarter of all status offenders except liquor law violations. White juveniles were overrepresented in liquor law violations cases and underrepresented in the other three status offense categories.

Table 1-2.
Percentage of Status Offense Cases by Gender 1985–2002

Gender	Status Offense			
	Runaway	Truancy	Ungovernability	Liquor
Males	42%	56%	54%	77%
Females	58%	44%	46%	23%

Source: Juvenile Court Statistics 1985–2002

Table 1-3
Race and Status Offenders 1985–2002

Race	Status Offense			
	Runaway	Truancy	Ungovernability	Liquor
White	73%	67%	71%	87%
Black	23%	29%	27%	8%
Other Races	3%	4%	2%	6%

Source: Juvenile Court Statistics 1985–2002

Adjudication

While the vast majority of all status offense cases are either handled informally or are dismissed once they get to the formal processing stage, in most cases where a petition is filed as a status offense, the youth was adjudicated. Across offenses, younger juveniles were more likely than older juveniles to result in adjudication. As Table 1-4 shows, from 1985 to 2002, the data tends to indicate that runaways were the least likely of all status offenses to be adjudicated. This may be due to the limited options available for other types of offenders as well as greater societal concerns about underage drinking, truancy and ungovernability.

As seen in Table 1-5, when adjudication does occur, a variety of outcomes are possible. Among the runaway cases, about 27%, were

Table 1-4.
Percentage of Adjudicated Cases by Offense 1985–2002

Offense	Adjudicated Per 1,000 cases	Not Adjudicated
Runaway	46% (459)	54%(541)
Truancy	63%(629)	37%(371)
Ungovernability	63%(625)	37%(375)
Liquor Law Violations	63%(630)	37%(370)

Source: Juvenile Court Statistics 1985–2002

Table 1-5.
Percentage of Adjudicated Sanctions 1985–2002

	Placed	Probation	Other Sanction	Released
Runaway	26.5%	61.4%	8.0%	3.9%
Truancy	10.8%	77.5%	9.6%	1.9%
Ungovernability	25.6%	65.7%	6.5%	2.0%
Liquor Violations	7.7%	57.4%	33.1%	1.5%

Source: Juvenile Court Statistics 1985–2002

placed in some type of facility or were referred to a social service agency, and 61% placed on probation. About 11% of truancy cases were adjudicated and approximately 25% of ungovernability cases, resulted in placement in residential facilities. Formal probation still remained the disposition of choice for these types of offenses.

Detention

Few petitioned youth charged with status offenses were held in detention. Those involved in truancy were the least likely to be detained at some point in their case, while youth involved in runaway cases were most likely to be detained. Moreover, when detention is the preferred option, males and females appear to be treated similarly (see Table 1-6).

Table 1-6.
Percentage of Status Offenders Detained 1985–2002

	Male	Female
Runaway	18%	16%
Ungovernability	10%	10%
Liquor	8%	6%
Truancy	4%	3%

Source: Juvenile Court Statistics 1985–2002

Table 1-7.
Percentage of Status Offenders Detained by Race 1985–2002

	White	Black	Other
Runaway	17%	16%	17%
Ungovernability	10%	10%	11%
Liquor	7%	14%	7%
Truancy	3%	4%	4%

Source: Juvenile Court Statistics 1985–2002

Between 1985 and 2002, the percentages of runaways detained rose to 17% and governability increased to 10%, with liquor law violations remaining the same and truancy rising from 1% to 3%. Similarly, the percentage of younger and older runaways increased to 17% while ungovernability cases saw a moderate increase. Truancy cases remained low, about 3% while liquor law violations based on age remained the same.

Like the distribution relating to gender, of those status offenders detained, racial differences disappear as well (see Table 1-7). That is, with the exception of African Americans who were detained for liquor violations, there appears to be no racial differences in detained status offenders.

The Variability of Treating Status Offending

While the goal of separating status offenses from more serious forms of delinquency may result in a minimization of a negative label, for all practical purposes, the distinction does not really affect the way the child is treated by the system. There is also a great deal of variability in how states treat status offenders in terms of whether or not they handle the case informally. Although status offenders are usually not detained or incarcerated with delinquents, they can be transferred to secure facilities if they are repeatedly unruly or considered uncontrollable. Some states are more likely to prosecute status offenses formally in the juvenile court while others handle most cases informally. Within individual states, some courts make a habit of prosecuting status offenders and others will divert most cases to treatment institutions (Stahl et al. 2005).

The Debate over Status Offenders: What to Do with Them?

More than two decades ago, the National Council on Crime and Delinquency an influential, privately funded think tank, recommended removing status offenders from the juvenile court. These calls for reform prompted a number of states to experiment with replacing juvenile court jurisdiction over most status offenders with community-based treatment programs.

However, as was mentioned, juvenile court judges strongly resist removal of status jurisdiction. They believe that reducing their authority over children leads to limiting juvenile court jurisdiction to only the most hard core offenders and interferes with their ability to help youths before they get into serious trouble. Their concerns are fueled by research that shows that many status offenders, especially runaways living on the street, have serious emotional problems and engage in a variety of self-destructive behaviors (Flowers 2001).

Those who favor removing status offenders from juvenile court authority charge that their experience with the legal system further stigmatizes already troubled youths, exposes them to the influence of "true" delinquents, and enmeshes them in the system that cannot really help them. Judges appear to be caught in the middle of a difficult situation. Some view status offenders as youth who need discipline and accountability. Consequently, a more punitive approach might be warranted. Other judges who focus less on punishment (which is questionable in terms of its effectiveness), discover that states have not really addressed the problem of status offenders and do not have programs in which to place the child. The lack of resources or programs, coupled with a general public that is demanding a more punitive approach to unlawful behavior (however it may be defined), leaves judges with few options.

Some experts have argued that not only does society have an obligation to provide help to status offenders, the juvenile court is the only way to force repeat offenders into compliance. Although it is recognized that a court appearance can produce negative stigma, the taint may be less important than the need for treatment.

On the other hand, compliance may not really be necessary for some offenders. Research shows that a majority of youth routinely engage in behaviors that currently qualify as status offenses (Stahl et al. 2005). Underage smoking, drinking, and truancy, as well as teen sex have become relatively commonplace. Experts contend that it makes little sense to have the juvenile court intervene into the lives of kids who are caught in what has become routine teenage behavior. In contrast, juvenile court jurisdiction over status offenders may be defended if the youths' offending patterns are similar to those of delinquents. The essential question in determining the court's role is whether or not the youths' current offense only the tip of their social iceberg, or are they actually non-criminal youths who need only the loving hand of a substitute parent figure interested in their welfare?

The debate over whether or not courts should retain jurisdiction over status offenses ignores or minimizes the importance of the different types of status offenders, some of whom are similar to delinquents while others are quite different in their motives and intentions. It might be more realistic to divide status offenders into three groups: first time status offenders, chronic status offenders, and those with both a delinquent record and a status offender's record. The fact that many young offenders have mixed records indicates that these legal categories are not entirely independent. Status offenders that are "pure" first timers are quite different from serious delinquents. A juvenile court experience can be harmful to them and could escalate the frequency and seriousness of their law violating behavior.

Repeat status offenders are also different from traditional delinquents. The reasons children run away from home do not change simply because the child has been arrested and court ordered to stop doing it. Thus, many repeat offenders are simply reacting to their environmental situations, some of which are intractable. However, despite the fact that the youth violated a valid court order, they are still not the same type of offender as the traditional delinquent. In sum, the difficulties in parceling out the types of offenders has resulted in an oversimplification of the problems and issues surrounding status offending. To treat them as delinquents only ensures that they will be appear in juvenile court at a later date and met with more punishment, creating a tragic cycle where the child is traumatized by their families as well as by society.

The next chapter explores the phenomenon of runaways, with an eye towards explaining the reasons for this activity as well as some of the traumatic consequences that result from life on the street. Clearly there are connections between runaway behavior and homelessness and this chapter will explore that connection. It will also include a description of some of the high-risk behaviors runaways engage in to survive. This includes such activities as prostitution and substance abuse. Chapter Three examines the is a wealth of evidence that demonstrates the connection between truancy and more serious forms of delinquency. While not a causal link, truancy is a gateway activity to more systematic forms of delinquency. Chapter Four examines ungovernability and curfew violations and their overall effectiveness in reducing delinquency. Chapter Five explores underage drinking, one of the most dangerous teenage activities, while in Chapter Six the problems associated with underage smoking are addressed. Chapter Seven concludes this book with a discussion of the likely future of the treatment of status offenders.

References

Brennan, T., Huizinga, D., and Elliott, D. S. 1978. *The Social Psychology of Runaways.* Lexington, MA: Lexington Books.

Bruchey, S. (ed.). 1999. *The Impact of Multiple Childhood Trauma on Homeless and Runaway Adolescents.* New York: Garland Publishing.

Department of Commerce, U.S. Census Bureau. 2006. Facts for Features. *Oldest Baby Boomers Turn 60.* Washington, DC: U.S. Government Printing Office.

Flowers, R. B. 2001. *Runaway Kids and Teenage Prostitution.* Westport, CT: Praeger.

Handler, J. F. and Zatz, J. (eds.) 1982. *Neither Angels Nor Thieves: Studies in Deinstitutionalization of Status Offenders.* Washington, DC: National Academy Press.

Hutzler, J. 1982. *Juvenile Court Jurisdiction over Children's Conduct: 1982 Comparative Analysis of Juvenile and Family Codes and National Standards.* Pittsburgh: National Center for Juvenile Justice.

IT Management. 2006. "Generation X for Dummies." www.eweek .com/article.

Maxon, C. and Klein, M. 1997. *Responding to Troubled Youth.* New York: Oxford University Press.

NAS Recruitment Communication. 2006. *Generation Y: The Millennias, Ready or Not, Here They Come.*

Schaffner, L. 1993. *Teenage Runaways.* Berkeley, CA: University of California Press.

Seigel, L., Welsh, B. C. and Senna, J. J. 2005. *Juvenile Delinquency: Theory, Practice and Law.* 9th edition. Belmont, CA: Wadsworth.

Stahl, A. L.; Puzzanchera, C.; Sladky, A.; Finnegan, T. A.; Tierney, N.; Snyder, H. N. 2005. *Juvenile Court Statistics Report.* Pittsburgh: National Center for Juvenile Justice.

Steinhart, D. J. 1996. "Status Offenses," *The Juvenile Court* 6(3), Winter.

Tyler, J. Segady, T. and Austin, S. 2000. "Parental Liability Laws: Rational, Theory, and Effectiveness." *Social Science Journal* 37:79–97.

Zemke, R., Raines, C. and Filipczak, B. 2000. *Generations at Work: Managing the Clash of Veterans, Boomers and Xers and Nexters in your Workplace.* New York: American Management Association.

Shadow Kids:
Runaways in the U.S.

Sammy is a sixteen year old boy who spends his days sitting with other students in classrooms at a local college in a small city in the southeastern part of the U.S. He sleeps in class and later decides to hang out at the beach where many tourists congregate. Sammy is dressed like most kids his age, which is to say he looks indistinguishable from thousands of teens. After panhandling money for food and cigarettes, Sammy finds an empty bench in the park near the beach. On some nights he wanders into the warehouse district of the city and sleeps in one of the many abandoned buildings while other nights he trades sex for shelter and food. Sammy thinks that living on the street is preferable to anything he encountered at home, where he was abused by his stepfather. However the likelihood of Sammy surviving the streets is low. Some kids like Sammy find housing in a local shelter for street youth or end up returning home. However, the circumstances surrounding why Sammy left home in the first place will inevitably resurface, likely leading to another episode of running away.

Each year as many as 2 million children leave home without a destination in mind. Tens of thousands of other children are pushed out of the house or abandoned by parents or guardians (National Incidence Studies of Missing, Abducted, Runaway, and Throwaway Children 2005). Caretakers may be aware of where the youth are located, but do not want to find them and bring them back home. Since not all runaways leave home due to family problems, some youth prefer to be on their own because of the independence they feel. However rarely do they find a better life in the streets. Most become involved in a cycle of poverty, drugs, prostitution, and various forms of victimization including STDs and crime. This chapter offers insight into the various reasons for running away and for those who don't return home, why they remain mired in this cycle of despair.

Definition of Runaways, Throwaways, and Homeless Youth

The term *homeless youth* is often used as an umbrella term for a large variety of young people including, runaways, throwaways, and homeless, or street kids. Many different definitions and criteria are used to describe these young people and they frequently overlap and are not mutually exhaustive or exclusive. There is even a wide range of disagreement as to what constitutes a young person. While most people tend to use under the age of 18 as the main criteria for status offenses, when it comes to homeless youth, it can also include ages ranging from 12 to 21.

In addition, part of the problem of defining runaway behavior is perception: while many youth may interpret their situation as one in which they have been thrown away, their caretakers may see it as more of a runaway episode (Hammer, Finkelhor, & Sedlak 2002). A third problem relating to understanding runaway behavior relates to the varying criteria official agencies use to qualify certain behaviors (van Wormer 2003). According to the U.S. Department of Health and Human Services, a runaway is a youth who is away from home without the permission of his or her parents or legal guardian at least overnight (see also Bass 1995). From a legislative point of view, The Runaway and Homeless Youth Act defines a *homeless youth* as one who is "not more than 21 years of age for whom it is not possible to live in a safe environment with a relative and who has no other safe alternative living arrangement" (42 U.S.C. 5732a.).

While there is no official definition of a *throwaway youth*, it is generally understood to be a young person who either is asked to leave home by a parent or other adult in the household or who is away from home overnight and prevented from returning home (Hammer, et al. 2002). As Ringwalt, Greene and Robertson (1998) have found, a throwaway can either be a youth who has been kicked out of their home for acting inappropriately or someone who has been abandoned. Ringwalt, Greene and Robertson (1998) also found that nearly half of youth living in shelters and on the street had a throwaway experience. In addition, youth with throwaway experiences were three to six times as likely as those without such an experience to have spent a night away from home because of family conflict, abuse, neglect, or because they felt unwelcome or unwanted.

The term *street youth* has been used to refer to those who reside in high-risk, nontraditional locations, such as under bridges, in abandoned buildings, or vehicles. The definition of the National Center for Homeless Education Unaccompanied and Homeless Youth defines street youth as "those who run away or who are indefinitely or intermittently homeless and spend a significant amount of time on the street or in other areas that increase their risk for sexual abuse, sexual exploitation, prostitution, or drug abuse (see also Moon, et al. 2001; Auerswald & Eyre 2002).

A Typology of Runaways

In trying to get a sense of the different types of runaways, a number of estimates suggest that some runaways were conceptualized as "voluntary missing." This helped to distinguish them from abducted and lost children. However, as the National Incidence Studies of Missing, Abducted, Runaway, and Throwaway Children, (NISMART-1) discovered, children who leave home often do so as a results of family conflict. In these instances, the term "voluntary" does not apply and is a bit misleading. Instead, NISMART-1 used the term thrown away youth to describe young people who were forced out of their homes or were refused permission to return (Finkelhor, Hotaling and Sedlak 1990).

NISMART-1, which is based on three components: the National Household Survey of Adult Caretakers, the National Household Survey of Youth, and the Juvenile Facilities Study, identified three different types of runaways. *Broad Scope Runaways* are defined as juveniles who leave or stay away from home without permission for at least one night. An exception to this are teenagers, age fifteen or older, who have permission to be out, but do not return home at the agreed upon time. NISMART stipulates that two nights are necessary for teens in such situations to be considered Broad Scope runaways.

Policy Focal Runaways are defined as minors who, along with fitting into the broad scope definition, are also endangered due to not having a familiar and safe place to stay. An example would be a youth who leaves home and spends time on the street, in a car, or in a shelter. The extreme conditions individuals in this category face make them the most noted by policy makers. It is also this group that garners the attention of law enforcement officials.

Runaway Gestures are defined as youth who leave home only for a matter of hours. This also includes runaways who leave a "runaway note." It also includes older teens that stay out overnight without permission. While this may be indicative of family issues and problems, this group is typically omitted from national figures on the incidence of runaways(Finkelhor, Hotaling and Sedlak 1990).

There is also a distinction made in NISMART between youth who run away from home and those who are referred to as *Non-Household Runaways*. These include those children who run away from institutions, group homes, or other facilities, such as hospitals, foster homes or boarding schools. According to the National Runaway Switchboard (2001), many youth who run away from home only do so for a short while, but do so long enough to meet the definition of a runaway. It is estimated that 40% of teens who leave home remain away anywhere from one to three days (Flowers 2001). The data also indicates that more than half of runaway youth believed that their home crisis could not be resolved by social service agencies.

While NISMART-1 made a distinction between runaways and throwaways, analysis revealed that many youth have episodes of both kinds of experiences. Additionally, the distinction between whether a youth was a throwaway or a runaway depended on whether researchers asked the youth or the caretaker. During the second wave of the study, NISMART-2, the distinction between runaways and throwaways was omitted and youth in this category were counted as part of a larger group called "runaway/throwaway." The emphasis in NISMART-2 was not so much which category a youth belonged to as the characteristics of the episode that led to them being put at risk.

According to NISMART-2, which included data collected from 1997 to 1999 (the year for which the most recent data is available), there are an estimated 1,682,900 youth who had a runaway episode. Of these an estimated 37% were "caretaker missing" youth, or when parents or guardians report youth missing, while 21% were reported missing to police or a missing children's agency for the purpose of locating them. Most runaway youth, 68%, were older teens between the ages of 15–17. About 28% were in the 12–14 age group and 4% were between the ages of 7 and 11.

Runaway and throwaway youth were equally divided between boys and girls and did not come disproportionately from any of the major racial or ethnic categories. About 57% of runaways/throwaways were White, compared to 17% who were African American. About 15% were Hispanic, and the remaining 12% were classified as Other or unknown.

More runaway/throwaway episodes occurred during the summer and about a quarter of runaways/throwaways traveled more than 50 miles from home. About 77% of runaways were gone less than one week and only 7% were gone more than one month. NISMART also reported that virtually all of the runaway children returned home by the time the study data was collected. Less than one percent, only 0.4%, had not returned home.

While there are a host of risk factors for runaway/throwaway youth, NISMART lists 17, the most common was physical or sexual abuse. The second most common factor was substance abuse. An estimated 39,000 runaways were at risk of sexual exploitation either by assault, an attempted assault, the youth was with someone known to be sexually abusive, or the youth engaged in sexual activity for money, drugs, food, or shelter.

The police were only contacted about a third of the time; in many cases the most common reasons for police contact was to help locate a missing youth. The police typically came in contact with runaway youth by arrest for suspicious or criminal activity. This is reflected in the Uniform Crime Report, where, in 2005, there were 108,954 arrests for running away and 3,764 arrests for suspicion. This does not take into account other criminal activity for which a youth was arrested but does not offer insight into whether or not they were runaways/throwaways.

Problems in Studying Runaways and Homeless Youth

As difficult as it is to define runaways, throwaways, street kids, or homeless youth, their hidden nature makes accurately counting them even more problematic (Raleigh-DuRoff 2004). Not only are there tremendous barriers to accurately estimating the size of such a changing population, the majority of methods for developing such estimates are flawed (Link, Phelan, Breshahan, Stueve, Moore, & Susser 1995). Compared to homeless adults and families, homeless youth have fewer shelters available (Wilder 2005). Many avoid shelters and other service providers, and those who live on the street often avoid researchers whom they may mistake for social service workers (Robertson & Clark, 1995; Ringwalt, Greene, & Robertson, 1998; Taylor, Lydon, Bougie, & Johannsen 2004).

One of the reasons estimates of the runaway and homeless youth population vary is that many are based on point prevalence methods that rely on a count done during a specified time interval. These estimates are biased toward describing the chronically homeless, but since youth homelessness is usually more periodic, "estimates of annual prevalence and incidence are biased downward" (Ringwalt, Greene, Robertson, & McPheeters 1998:1326).

Survival Strategies: Crime and Sex Work

According to the National Clearinghouse on Families and Youth, a great many runaway youth are actually throwaways or end up homeless. Although more than half of all runaways are girls, most of those living on the streets are boys (see also Office of Juvenile Justice and Delinquency Prevention 2005).

Some agencies estimate that one in seven youths will leave home by the age of 18 (National Runaway Switchboard, 2001). For many, running away is not limited to one episode; they may run many times. What begins with an initial run to a friend's house may lead to chronic runaway behavior. Once on the street, the youth are often in places where criminal activity occurs (Biehal & Wade 1999). The result is that runaways can become offenders or victims of violence. Runaways are ideal targets for offenders because they rarely report crimes committed against them (Baron 1997).

As was mentioned, because running away is considered a status offense, this behavior would not be considered criminal if committed by an adult. However, police officers do arrest runaways, although the reasons for it may stem more from paternalism than the fact that they have committed a serious crime. According to the Uniform Crime Reports, in 2005 there were approximately 109,000 arrests for running away. This comprised about 7% of all arrests for juveniles. The relationship of running away to crime is perhaps more noticeable in terms of survival techniques, which can often lead to arrests. Examples include prostitution, drug dealing, and burglary. In addition, some runaways are charged with vandalism and criminal trespass when they attempt to secure housing in abandoned buildings.

According to the National Runaway Switchboard, runaway youth typically begin with panhandling as a survival strategy but they will inevitably turn to the illegal economy such as prostitution, pornography, shoplifting and other crimes. According to Johnson (2006) many homeless and runaway youth engage in a host of criminal activities to survive, including trading sex for food, shelter, money, or drugs. However, survival sex is usually reserved as a last resort strategy and often serves as an indication of the sense of desperation many homeless youth feel (see also Hagan and McCarthy 1997; Flowers 2001). Other youth trade sex due to exploitation or manipulation (Biglan et al.1995). Although relatively little is known about the actual circumstances surrounding survival sex, some studies have indicated that it tends to occur infrequently, with perhaps 20% of homeless youth engaging in the activity (Beech, Meyers, and Beech 2002; Van Leeuwen et al. 2004). Not surprisingly, street youth are more likely to trade sex than teens living in shelters. Males are more likely to trade sex for money while females are more likely to do it in exchange for alcohol or drugs (Greene et al. 1999; Kral et al. 1997). As was mentioned, some teens voluntarily engage in survival sex, particularly those that have been on the street and have friends who engage in this activity, but some youth are coerced into it. Some youth, for example, may be exploited by an adult who initially provided care for them, only to demand payment in the form of sex in exchange (Hagan and McCarthy 1997). Others were "turned out" by their boyfriends who are then paid by clients (Tyler et al. 2000; Hagan and McCarthy 1997). Anecdotal evidence suggests that in some of these situations, the girlfriend gets nothing from the transaction (Johnson 2006). While less is known about the circumstances surrounding survival sex as well as whether or not the decision to engage in this activity is voluntary, the reality is that many homeless and runaway youth are at substantial physical and psychological risks (Tyler et al. 2000).

Psychological Effects of Runaway Behavior

There are a host of risks runaways face, some of which are quite severe: malnutrition, psychological disorders, HIV infection and other sexually transmitted diseases, unwanted pregnancies, drug and alcohol abuse, robbery, and sexual and physical assault have all been found in high proportions among runaways. One study found the rates of major depression, conduct disorder, and posttraumatic stress were three times as high among runaway youth as their peers. (Robertson 1989). HIV may be up to 10 times as prevalent among runaway and homeless youth than for other adolescents (Stricof, Novick, and Kennedy 1990).

A number of studies dealing with runaway youth center around health issues and substance abuse. Homeless youth also exhibit high rates of psychological symptoms such as depression, anxiety, conduct disorders (MacLean, et al. 1999; Thompson, et al., 2002), post-traumatic stress, poor school adjustment, delinquent acting out, and aggressive behaviors (Cauce, et al., 2000). Up to 24% of females and

16% of males could have post-traumatic stress disorder (PTSD) (Cauce et al. 2000). One of the most common and serious problems of youth homelessness is low self-esteem (Pearce 1995; Pears & Noller 1995). Feeling rejected and abandoned can lead to extreme loneliness and hopelessness (Rotherham-Borus et al. 1996).

Other influences to leave stem from problems outside the family, such as difficulties with school, teachers, peers, pregnancy, sexual orientation, and mental health issues (Hagan & McCarthy 1997; Rotheram-Borus, Parra, et al. 1996). Some studies have found a high rate of Attention Deficit Hyperactivity Disorder (ADHD) among homeless youth (Cauce et al. 2000; National Health Care for the Homeless Council 2002; Stanford et al. 1999; van Wormer 2003). ADHD may be a result instead of a cause of homelessness or it could be that when schools fail to meet the needs of students with ADHD, they are more prone to failure and dropping out which then leads to poverty and a greater possibility of homelessness (van Wormer 2003).

Quite a few studies have documented that health risks are significantly higher for runaways than for their housed counterparts especially risks related to their sexual behavior, such as AIDS, other sexually transmitted diseases, (Rew 1996; Taylor et al. 2004), and teen pregnancies (Kipke et al.1997). Over half of runaway and homeless adolescent females report having been pregnant at least once, with more than a quarter reporting two or more pregnancies (Halcon and Lifson 2004).

Domestic Violence

High levels of domestic violence in the family are also significantly associated with runaways being mistreated on the street (Sullivan and Knutson 2000; Whitbeck et al. 1997). Many researchers have found high rates of victimization among street youth, with reports of abuse ranging as high as 81% (Baron 2003). Additionally, being the victim of one type of abuse, particularly sexual abuse, increases the likelihood of being the victim of another form of it (Craig and Hodson 1998). These youths endure so many different types of maltreatment it is difficult to establish a clear-cut link between one type of maltreatment and a specific behavior, but most who experience physical and sexual abuse suffer the same problems as those who experience one or the other, only to a greater extent (Baron 2003).

Street youth often come from violent families. Research suggests that being the victim of violence increases violent behavior on the street because abusive families have trained their children in violent and anti-social behavior (Baron and Hartnagel 1997, 1998; Cauce et al. 2000; Paradise et al. 2001). Fleisher (1995) says abuse and rejection lead youth to develop a defensive, fear-based belief that people cannot be trusted and will not help them; this belief system also makes youth more willing to use violence and intimidation.

Social Isolation

Contrary to popular beliefs, Bao, Whitbeck, and Hoyt (2000) contend that many runaway youth have strong social supports and some even maintain family ties, particularly if abuse was not involved. Although it is commonly assumed that the social environment of youth living on the street encourages unsafe and criminal activities (Johnson, Aschkenasy, Hervers, and Gillenwater 1996), some studies found that youths often end up with other homeless kids in a surrogate street family formed for the sake of survival and protection against violence (Fleisher 1995; Hagan and McCarthy 1997). The downside of this is that when homeless youth band together on the street they may no longer have the opportunity to benefit from positive influences outside their network (Fleisher 1995).

On the other hand, some research shows that street youth are generally unlikely to form a close social group, instead spending their time with one or two others and the few close relationships they do have most likely preceded their homelessness (Baron, Kennedy et al., 2001; Fleisher 1995). While it is not clear how social relationships are formed, there is evidence to suggest that, as Baron, Kennedy and Forde (2001) point out, those without a network of support reported more current illicit drug use, multiple sex partners, and survival sex. This seems to suggest that if the youth becomes connected to a group that engages in risky behaviors, they too will follow suit.

Runaways, Foster Care, and Incarceration

The disproportionate representation of former foster care children among the runaway and homeless population has been well documented. According to a nationwide study of runaway youths, more than one-third had been in foster care the year before they took to the streets. More than one out of five youths who arrive at a shelter come directly from a foster or group home, with 38% saying they had been in foster care at some time during the previous year (Robertson and Toro 1998). Some experts estimate that almost half of youth who leave foster care become homeless within a year (*San Diego Daily Transcript* 1996). As many as 70% of homeless youth have spent time in a foster home, group home, or other residential facility (Administration for Children and Families 1995; Wilder Research 2005), and over 22% with foster care experience are homeless for one day or more after the age of 18 (Casey Family Programs 2005).

In New York City, a study determined that 25%–50% of the young men in homeless shelters were former foster children (Oreskes 1987). The long-term and cyclical effects of foster care were revealed in a study by the Institute for Children and Poverty (2004), where it was discovered that homeless families whose heads of households grew up in foster care were more likely to have their marriage end in divorce and to have their children placed in foster care. Clearly the deleterious effects of foster care as a child have implications even for those individuals who manage to get out of the system, off the streets, and create something of a normal life for themselves.

Not only is there a link between the effects of foster care, runaway behavior and homelessness, but incarceration is also a likely outcome for some individuals. For instance, one study of former foster children found that one-fourth had been homeless, 40% were on public assistance, and half were unemployed. In another study in Connecticut, an estimated 75% of youths in the state's criminal justice system were once in foster care (Bayles and Cohen 1995). Still another study found that 80% of prisoners in Illinois spent time in foster care as children (Azar 1995). It is fairly clear that the linkages between these childhood experiences and damaging adult conduct are connected.

Why Runaways Leave Home

While there seems to be no typical single cause to explain why teens run away or become homeless, most of the reasons given can be grouped into three broad, inter-related categories: family problems (which include the behaviors of both parents and youth), economic problems, and residential instability (National Coalition for the Homeless 1999; van Wormer 2003; Wilder Research 2005).

Family Problems

Family conflict is central for youth because they are usually financially, emotionally, and legally dependent on their parents. Research has shown that the majority of those who leave home prematurely do so either to escape dysfunctional or abusive family situations (including physical, sexual, or psychological abuse), or they are coerced into leaving by their parents or other adults in their household (National Coalition for the Homeless 1999; Powers, Eckenrode, and Jaklitsch 1990; Whitbeck and Simons 1990; 1993; Wilder Research 2005). As was mentioned, some studies show that those with poor family relations have difficulty forming relationships with service providers, which makes it difficult or impossible to access all the existing services that could support them in transitioning to a more stable lifestyle (Kipke et al. 1997).

There is a clear relationship between physical and sexual abuse of youth and their subsequent homelessness (Bao, Whitbeck, and Hyot 2000). In addition to violence and abuse, other family-related factors that influence young people to leave home include neglect, parental substance abuse (Hagan and McCarthy 1997; Rotheram-Borus et al.1996; Whitbeck and Hoyt 1999), and parental control issues (Whitbeck and Hoyt 1999).

Economic Problems

For some youth, economic problems may lead to running away or homelessness (Hagan and McCarthy 1997). One study of over 1,200 homeless youth reported that about 40% were from families that received public assistance or lived in public housing (Administration for Children and Families 1995). Also, low wages leads some families to ask their children to leave home (van Wormer 2003). This often results in the aforementioned throwaway phenomenon.

Residential Instability

Residential instability is another factor contributing to the homelessness of youths (Hagan and McCarthy 1997; Wright et al. 1998). Wright et al. (1998) say homelessness is a stage of residential instability that is often preceded by living in doubled-up housing. It can also be related to economic problems in that families cannot always afford to care for their children, leaving the family vulnerable to homelessness. As a result of family conflict or economic constraints, youth are sometimes forced to seek other housing alternatives, most of which are precarious. Wright et al. (1998) consider youth to be living in doubled-up housing when they have no other place to go and are temporarily taken in by others.

Programs for Runaway, Throwaway and Homeless Youth

Since 1974, Congress has funded three programs under the Runaway and Homeless Youth Act. In 2005, with $84 million in funding, these three programs—street outreach, basic or walk-in centers (shelters), and transitional living—operate in hundreds of communities around the country. Street outreach workers try to pass on information to young people living on the streets to keep them safe and healthy and show them ways to improve their circumstances. They also refer young people to medical and mental health treatment, counseling, and other resources and try to bring some into shelters for more intensive help.

Walk-in centers offer short-term shelter, food, clothing, and medical assistance and counseling to reunify families when possible and appropriate. Staff can also try to place a young person elsewhere or prepare him or her to live independently. For homeless youth 16–21 who are unable to return home, transitional living programs provide housing and comprehensive social services aimed at achieving self-sufficiency. Some clients are single parents.

The runaway and homeless youth agency that was the model for many others is *The Bridge*, in Boston, Massachusetts, which started doing street outreach in Harvard Square in 1970. The Bridge is not a shelter in the traditional sense. Upon finding a runaway youth, workers try to find them a safe place for a few nights in the homes of local families. Services provided by The Bridge include a transitional day program, a medical van, a dental clinic, substance abuse counseling, family work and advocacy, and a pre-employment program. Staffed by 45 employees and 200 volunteers, mostly professionals helping in their fields, The Bridge serves about 2,000 kids annually. Under its two-phase transitional living program, 34 young people, including single mothers, can stay in communal residences and shared apartments for up to three and a half years (Slavin 2005; Lindsay 1994).

One promising avenue in seeking to decrease the problems associated with homeless youth is through the school system. According to Rafferty (1995), runaway and homeless children want to go to school and think their education is very important. It is also a strong predictor of the ability to overcome poverty and become independent; without education, homeless children may never have the opportunity to acquire many critical life skills (Nunez 1995). Some street kids survive by finding an oasis in the midst of the turmoil, and for some kids that is going to school (Slavin 2001). Unfortunately, research also shows that up to three quarters of older homeless youths drop out of school (Cauce et al. 2000). In one study, formerly homeless youth reported that leaving school was a turning point in their lives and that their situations worsened afterward (Lindsey and Williams 2002).

Summary

As many as 2 million children leave home without a destination in mind each year in this country, while tens of thousands of other children are pushed out or abandoned by their parents or guardians.

While many of those return home eventually, for a segment of this population, life on the streets becomes their only option. Part of the problem of understanding runaways is that the definitions vary considerably and the behaviors youth engage in while on the street can lead to other labels. The terms throwaway youth, homeless youth, street kids, and others are often synonymous with runaway behavior. While running away remains a status offense, for which the police sometimes arrest youth, other activities, such as shoplifting, robbery, and survival sex in the form of prostitution become a reality for many street kids. These activities, as well as life on the streets in general, place teens in a precarious physical and psychological situation. Runaways and homeless youth are at great risk for malnutrition, psychological disorders, HIV infection and other sexually transmitted diseases, unwanted pregnancies, drug and alcohol abuse and various forms of criminal victimization. They are also more likely to suffer from depression, low self-esteem, and post-traumatic stress disorder.

A number of factors cause youth to runaway, a large part of which involves physical and sexual abuse by parents, caregivers or guardians. Many kids who end up on the street have also spent time in foster care. This is likely due to the dysfunctional nature of their families, which is also a risk factor for running away and homelessness.

While the federal government has recently enacted legislation to assist runaway and street youth, most of the programs are only stop-gap measures that try to provide comfort to teens living on the street and to try to get them to return home. As a result, their overall effectiveness is limited.

References

Auerswald, C. L., & Eyre, S. L. 2002. "Youth homelessness in San Francisco: A life cycle approach." *Social Science & Medicine*, 54, 1497–1512.

Azar, B. "Foster Care Has Bleak History," *APA Monitor*, (November, 1995)

Bao, W., Whitbeck, L., & Hyot, D. 2000. "Abuse, Support, and Depression among Homeless and Runaway Adolescents." *Journal of Health and Social Behavior,* 41, 408–420.

Baron, S. 1997. "Risky Lifestyles and the Link between Offending and Victimization." *Studies on Crime and Crime Prevention,* 6, 53–72.

Baron, S. 2003. "Street Youth Violence and Victimization." *Trauma, Violence, & Abuse,* 4(1), 22–44.

Baron, S., & Hartnagel, T. 1997. "Attributions, Affect and Crime: Street Youths' Reactions to Unemployment." *Criminology,* 35, 409–434.

Baron, S., Kennedy, L., & Forde, D. 2001. "Male Street Youths' Conflict: The Role of Background Subcultural and Situational Factors." *Justice Quarterly,* 18, 759–789.

Bass, D. 1995. "Runaways and Homeless Youths." *Encyclopedia of Social Work* 19th edition. Washington, DC: NASW Press.

Bayles, F. and Cohen, S. 1995. "Chaos Often the Only Parent for Abused or Neglected Children" (AP) *Los Angeles Times,* (April 30th.

Beech, B. M., Myers, L., and Beech, D. 2002. "Hepatitis B and C Infections Among Homeless Adolescents." *Family and Community Health* 25, 28–26.

Biehal, N., & Wade, J. 2002. "Going Missing from Residential and Foster Care: Linking Biographies and Contexts." *British Journal of Social Work,* 30, 211–225.

Biglan, A.; Noell, J.; Ochs, L.; Smolkowski, K.; and Metzler, C. 1995. "Does Sexual Coercion Play a Role in the High Risk Sexual Behavior of Adolescent and Young Adult Women?" *Journal of Behavioral Medicine* 18, 54–56.

Brooks, R., Milburn, N., Rotheram-Borus, M., & Witkin, A. 2004. "The System-of-Care for Homeless Youth: Perceptions of Service Providers." *Evaluation and Program Planning,* 27(4), 443–451.

Casey Family Programs. 2005. Improving Family Foster Care: Findings from the Northwest Foster Care Alumni Study. Retrieved June 11, 2007, from http://www.casey.org/NR/rdonlyres/4E1E 7C777624-4260-A253-92C5A6CB9E1/ 300/nw_alumni_study_full _apr2005.pdf.

Cauce, A., Paradise, M., Ginzler, J., Embry, L., Morgan, C., Lohr, Y., 2000. "The Characteristics of Mental Health of Homeless Adolescents: Age and Gender Differences." *Journal of Emotional and Behavioral Disorders*, 8(4): 230–239.

Craig, T., & Hodson, S. 1998. "Homeless Youth in London: Childhood Antecedents and Psychiatric Disorder." *Psychological Medicine*, 28, 1379–1388.

Ensign, J., & Bell, M. 2004. "Illness Experiences of Homeless Youth." *Qualitative Health Research*, 14(9), 1239–1254.

Fleisher, M.1995. *Beggars and Thieves.* Madison: University of Wisconsin Press.

Flowers, B. 2001. *Runaways and Teenage Prostitution.* Westport, CT: Praeger.

Greene, J., Ennett, S., & Ringwalt, C. 1999. "Prevalence and Correlates of Survival Sex among Runaway and Homeless Youth." *American Journal of Public Health*, 89(9): 1406–1409.

Hagan, J. and McCarthy, B. 1997. *Mean Streets: Youth Crime and Homelessness.* Cambridge, MA: Cambridge University Press. Institute for Children and Poverty.

Halcon, L., & Lifson, A. 2004. "Prevalence and Predictors of Sexual Risks among Homeless Youth." *Journal of Youth and Adoles*cence, 33(1): 71–80.

Hammer, H., Finkelhor, D., & Sedlak, A. 2002. Runaway/thrownaway Children: National Estimates and Characteristics. *National Incidence Studies of Missing, Abducted, Runaway and Thrownaway Children.*

Homes for the Homeless. 1993. *Homelessness: The Foster Care Connection.*

Johnson, K. A. 2006. "Trading Sex: Voluntary or Coerced? The Experiences of Homeless Youth." *Journal of Sex Research.*

Johnson, T., Aschkenasy, J., Herbers, M., & Gillenwater, S. 1996. "Self-Reported Risk Factors for AIDS among Homeless Youth." *AIDS Education and Prevention*, 8, 302–322.

Kipke, M., Montgomery, S., Simon, T., Unger, J., & Johnson, T. 1997. "Homeless Youth: Drug Use Patterns and HIV Risk Profiles According to Peer Affiliation." *AIDS and Behavior*, 1(4), 247–259.

Klein, J., Woods, A., Wilson, K., Prospero, M., Greene, J., & Ringwalt, C. 2000. "Homeless and Runaway Youth's Access to Healthcare." *Journal of Adolescent Health*, 27, 331–339.

Kral, A. H.; Molnar, B. E.; Booth, R. E.; and Watters, J. K. 1997. "Prevalence of Sexual Risk Behavior and Substance Abuse Among Runaway and Homeless Adolescents in San Francisco, Denver, and New York City." *International Journal of STD And AIDS*, 8, 109–117.

Kurtz, D., Lindsey, E., Jarvis, S., & Nackerud, L. 2000. "How Runaway and Homeless Youth Navigate Troubled Waters: The Role of Formal and Informal Helpers." *Child and Adolescent Social Work*, 17(5): 381–402.

Lindsey, D. 1994. *The Welfare of Children*. New York: Oxford University Press.

Lindsey, E., & Williams, N. 2002. "How Runaway and Homeless Youth Survive Adversity: Implications for School Social Workers and Educators." *School Social Work Journal*, 27(1): 1–21.

Link, B., Phelan, J., Breshahan, M., Stueve, A., Moore, R., & Susser, E. 1995. "Lifetime and Five-Year Prevalence of Homelessness in the United States: New Evidence on an Old Debate." *American Journal of Orthopsychiatry*, 65, 347–354.

MacLean, M., Embry, L., & Cauce, A. 1999. "Homeless Adolescents' Paths to Separation from Family: Comparison of Family Characteristics, Psychological Adjustment, and Victimization." *Journal of Community Psychology*, 27(2): 179–187.

Mallett, S., Rosenthal, D., Myers, P., Milvurn, N., & Rotheram-Borus, M. 2003. "Practicing Homelessness: A Typology Approach to Young People's Daily Routines." *Journal of Adolescence*, 27, 337–349.

McCaffrey, E. 1994. "Caught in a Twilight Zone," *San Diego Union-Tribune*, April 13th.

McKinney-Vento Homeless Assistance Act 42 U.S.C. 11301 Sec.101. Missing, Exploited, and Runaway Children Protection Act, P.L. 106-71, Section 387, 2000.

Moon, M., Binson, D., Page-Shafter, K., & Diaz, R. 2001. "Correlates of HIV Risk in a Random Sample of Street Youths in San Francisco." *Journal of the Association of Nurses in AIDS Care,* 12(6): 18–27.

National Alliance to End Homelessness. 2003. Runaway and Homeless Youth Act. Retrieved June 3, 2007, from http://www.endhomelessness.org/pol/rhya.html.

National Clearinghouse on Families and Youth. (1995). *Youth with Runaway, Throwaway, and Homeless Experiences: Prevalence, Drug Use, and Other At-Risk Behaviors.* Silver Spring, MD.

National Coalition for the Homeless, "Breaking the Foster Care—Homelessness Connection." Sept/Oct 1998.

National Runaway Switchboard. News and research. Retrieved June 3, 2007 from http://www.nrscrisisline.org/news.asp.

Noell, J., Rohde, P., Seeley, J., & Och, L. 2001. "Maltreatment among Runaway and Homeless Youth." *Child Abuse and Neglect,* 25(1): 137–148.

Nunez, R. 1995. *An American Family Myth: Every Child at Risk.* New York: Homes for the Homeless.

Office of Juvenile Justice and Delinquency Prevention (OJJDP), Washington, DC, *Fact Sheet on Missing Children: National Incidence Studies of Missing, Abducted, Runaway, and Thrownaway Children* (2005). National Network for Youths Runaway and Homeless Youth: Toolkit for Youth Workers.

Oreskes, M. 1987. "A System Overloaded: The Foster Care Crisis," *New York Times,* March 15th.

Paradise, M., Cauce, A., Ginzler, J., Wert, S. Wruck, K., & Brooker, M. 2001. "The Role of Relationships in Developmental Trajectories of Homeless and Runaway Youth." In B. Sarason & S. Duck (Eds.), *Personal Relationships: Implications for Clinical and Community Psychology* (pp. 159–179). New York: John Wiley.

Pearce, K. 1995. "Street Kids Need Us To: Special Characteristics of Homeless Youth." *Parks & Recreation*, 30(12): 16.

Pears, J., & Noller, P. 1995. "Youth Homelessness: Abuse, Gender, and the Life on the Streets." *Australian Journal of Social Issues*, 30(4): 405–424.

Powers, J., Eckenrode, J., & Jaklitsch, B. 1990. "Maltreatment among Runaway and Homeless Youth." *Child Abuse and Neglect*, 14(1): 87–98.

Raleigh-DuRoff, C. 2004. "Factors that Influence Adolescents to Leave or Stay Living on the Street." *Child and Adolescent Social Work Journal*, 21(6):561–572.

Ringwalt, C., Greene, J., & Robertson, M. 1998. "Familial Backgrounds and Risk Behaviors of Youth with Thrownaway Experiences." *Journal of Adolescence*, 21, 241–252.

Robertson, M., & Toro, P. 1998. "Homeless Youth: Research, Intervention, and Policy." In L. Fosburg & D. Dennis (Eds.), *Practical Lessons: The 1998 National Symposium on Homelessness Research*. Washington, DC: U.S. Department of Housing and Urban Development.

Robertson, M.J. (1989). *Homeless Youth in Hollywood: Patterns of Alcohol Use* (Report No. C51). Bethesda, MD: National Institute on Alcohol Abuse and Alcoholism.

Roman, P., & Wolfe, P. 1997. "The Relationship Between Foster Care and Homelessness." *American Public Welfare Association*, Winter, 4–10.

Rotheram-Borus, M., Mahler, K., Koopman, C., & Langabeer, K. 1996. "Sexual Abuse History and Associated Multiple Risk Behavior in Adolescent Runaways." *American Journal of Orthopsychiatry*, 66, 390–400.

Slavin, P. 2001. "Life on the Run, Life on the Streets." *Children's Voice* July.

Stricof, R.L.; Novick, L.F.; and Kennedy, J.T. (1990, November). HIV seroprevalence in facilities for runaway and homeless adolescents in four states: Florida, Texas, Louisiana, and New York. Paper presented at the Sixth International Conference on AIDS, San Francisco.

Sullivan, P., & Knutson, J. 2000. "The Prevalence of Disabilities and Maltreatment Among Runaway Children." *Child Abuse & Neglect*, 24(10):1275–1288.

Taylor, D., Lydon, J., Bougie, E., & Johannsen, K. 2004. "Street Kids": Toward an Understanding of their Motivational Context." *Canadian Journal of Behavioral Science*, 36(1), 1–16.

Thompson, S., Pollio, D., Constantine, J., Reid, D., & Nebbitt, V. 2002. "Short-term Outcomes for Youth Receiving Runaway and Homeless Shelter Services." *Research on Social Work Practice*, 12(5): 589–603.

Tyler, K., Hoyt, D., Whitbeck, L., & Cauce, A. 2001. "The Effects of High-risk Environment on Sexual Victimization of Homeless and Runaway Youth." *Violence and Victims*, 16, 441–455.

van Leeuwen, J. M.; Hopfer, C.; Hooks, S.; White, R.; Petersen, J.; and Pirkopf, J. 2004. "Snapshot of Substance Abuse Among Homeless and Runaway Youth in Denver." *Journal of Community Health* 29, 217–229.

van Wormer, R. 2003. "Homeless Youth Seeking Assistance: A Research-based Study from Duluth, Minnesota." *Child & Youth Forum*, 32(2): 89–103.

Whitbeck, L. B. and Hoyt, D. R. 1999. *Nowhere to Grow: Homeless and Runaway Adolescents and their Families.* New York: Aldine de Gruyter.

Wilder Research Center. 2005. *Homeless Youth in Minnesota: 2003 Statewide Survey of People Without Shelter.* St. Paul, MN: Wilder Research Center.

3

Truancy

When people think of students skipping school for the day, they typically do not think of it as a national problem with a host of social, economic, and political implications. However, every day hundreds of thousands of students are absent from school; many without an excuse. Although national data on truancy rates are unavailable, partly due to the fact that no uniform definition exists, many cities wrestle with the problem of truancy (Baker, Sigmon and Nugent 2001). In fact, so significant is the problem of truancy that a national review of discipline issues in public schools found that principals identified student absenteeism, class cutting, and tardiness as the top discipline problems on their campuses (Heaviside et al. 1998).

The implications for truancy extend far beyond the educational deficiencies for those students who miss school. Truancy has been identified as one of the most important gateway activities for additional problem behaviors. In fact, the U.S. Department of Education has stated that truancy is the most powerful predictor of juvenile delinquent behavior. Many studies have connected truancy to dropping out of school, teen pregnancy, substance abuse, gang involvement, and serious forms of delinquency (Puzzanchera, et al. 2003; Rosen and Dynlacht 1994; Huzinga, Loeber and Thornberry 1995; Rohrman 1993). There is also a link between truancy and adult problem behaviors, such as violence, marital problems, welfare dependency, chronic unemployment, adult crime, and incarceration (Dryfoos 1990; Snyder and Sickmund 1995; Catalano et al. 1998). With regard to demographic variables, a few trends are noteworthy. For instance, the relationship between race and truancy is not well established. Some data suggests that Whites are underrepresented in petitioned cases (Bell, Rosen, and Dynlacht 1994; Puzzanchera et al. 2003). Other studies have found that African Americans and Latinos consistently have the highest drop out rates of all categories of students (Kaufman, Alt, and Chapman 2001). Additionally, while the relationship between income and truancy is not well known, it is generally believed that students from lower income families have higher rates of truancy (Bell et al. 1994). Finally, there is some evidence that boys and girls are about evenly divided in the truancy statistics, with 15 years old as the peak age for truancy cases (Puzzanchera et al. 2003). However, while girls tend to demonstrate a slightly higher rate of absenteeism in high school than boys, the latter are more likely to become chronically truant, especially in the later grades (Allen-Meares, Washington and Welsh 2000).

With regard to juvenile crime, law enforcement officials have linked high rates of truancy to daytime burglary and vandalism. In Tacoma, WA, for instance, the police department reported that 1/3 of burglaries and 1/5 of aggravated assaults occurring between 8am and 1pm on weekdays were committed by juveniles. In Contra Costa County, CA, police reported that 60% of juvenile crime occurred between 8am and 3pm on weekdays (Baker, Sigmon and Nugent 2001).

According to the Office of Juvenile Justice and Delinquency Prevention (OJJDP), adults who were truant at an early age were much more likely (than those who were not truant) to have poorer physical and mental health statuses, lower paying jobs, a higher likelihood of living in poverty, more reliance on welfare support, and to have children who exhibit problem behaviors (Baker, Sigmon and Nugent 2001).

A related phenomenon worth mentioning consists of students who simply refuse to attend school despite any efforts made by parents, schools, or the courts. *School refusal* is defined as a psychological condition in which the child is reluctant (and often outright refuses) to go to school. Psychologists state that children suffering from school refusal tend to seek the comfort of home and to remain in close proximity to parental figures during school hours. They also tend to display visible and emotional outbursts at the prospect of attending school, yet do not seem to have any problems in controlling other behavior or aggressiveness. In addition to violent outbursts, some students also identify physical ailments at the thought of going to school, such as headaches, diarrhea, and stomach aches. While this disorder is more of an emotional reaction to leaving home than it is related to school per se, nevertheless, it has an impact on truancy (Berg 1997).

Finally, another dimension of truancy consists of students who are referred to as *push outs*. Virtually every state has implemented a series of challenging end of course tests that are required for graduation, which are part of a larger effort to improve public education. However, as more and more schools are being held accountable for educating today's youth, one strategy to ensure higher overall scores has been to convince poorly performing students that they should leave school. Critics of high stakes testing policies have charged that do-or-die exams prompt struggling students to drop out of school, either because they are discouraged by their failure to pass exams or because schools do not want their ratings decreased by lower scoring students (Rubin 2004). In other words, accountability testing has led some school districts to push students out of school illegally because of low test scores, low grades, chronic truancy, or other issues.

An example of pushing students out of school occurred in New York City. In January 2004, the New York City school system settled a federal lawsuit in which former students alleged that they had been pushed out of one of the city's high schools because of low grades, low test scores, and truancy. Under New York state law, students are entitled to attend public school until age 21. They can be legally expelled or suspended only for disruptive or violent behavior, not due to truancy, age, or poor academic performance (Rubin 2004). Part of the problem with accountability testing is that schools often fail to notify students of their right to return to classes and to offer them extra academic help. In the case of New York City, the school district failed to inform students they could return to school, told some students the district could no longer afford to keep them in the school, or simply failed to provide any academic assistance to improve their scores.

Truancy and the Criminal Justice System

As Bazemore, Stinchcomb and Leip (2004) point out, historically enforcing truancy laws was primarily a function of the court system. However, some legal experts note that in the 1970s, particularly landmark U.S. Supreme Court cases such as *In re Gault* as well as legislation, such as the Juvenile Justice and Delinquency Prevention Act of 1974, began to limit the Court's influence over status offenses such as truancy. Consequently, the problem increased, largely due to the lack of enforcement power that had been given to the courts.

By the end of the 1990s, truancy had become a focal point in the study and treatment of juveniles and policymakers returned to the more punitive approach by restoring to the courts the authority to hear cases. Treating truancy is similar to other offenses such as underage drinking, smoking, running away and the enforcement of juvenile curfews. That is, as society began to demand more in the way of accountability of its youth, an enforcement arm of the government was required to achieve compliance. This came at a time when "getting tough" on crime was a prevalent theme for all segments of society.

One might argue that there are essentially two schools of thought regarding truancy: the social work model and the social control model. In the social work model, the reasons for truancy stem largely from individual factors such as learning disabilities, family problems, and other psychological factors that prevent children from academic success, which, in turn, leads to truancy. The social control model contends that truancy is a symptom of a larger set of problems and that youth skip school for similar reasons as they commit other delinquent acts. Programs that focus on the intervention of the criminal justice system fall into this category and generally believe truants to be a public safety risk. Consequently, programs such as specialized truancy courts are designed to seek compliance and accountability of the youth rather than addressing the problems that cause them to be truant in the first place (Bazemore, Stinchcomb and Leip 2004).

This crime control model has become a standard feature of the treatment of truancy. In fact, the involvement of the criminal justice system in a school-related activity like truancy can be seen with the introduction of school resource officers (SROs). Initially, SROs were designed to provide educational opportunities (e.g. lectures, seminars) as well as safety and protection. However, as McElvain and Kposowa (2006) point out, this shift in philosophy can be seen in the role of SROs, the language used to describe criminal justice officials, and the range of activities within the school. It is also evident in schools' emphasis on rules and regulations within schools which focus on criminal activity.

For example, the language used to describe the role of the police within the schools has changed. What was once a "school resource officer" has now become "guards," "gang intelligence officers," or "drill instructors." Moreover, school officials and policymakers now describe the answer to problems like delinquency as "fighting" campus crime or "enforcing" school discipline. Moreover, while SROs were initially intended to bring an educational component to the schools, increasingly law enforcement activities have focused more on behavioral and crime control than pedagogy. In many schools SROs find themselves conducting more drug sweeps, surveillance, security checks, than giving lectures on the problems of drugs and teen pregnancy.

In short, the problems stemming from truancy are increasingly giving way to a form of accountability that puts less emphasis on the context in which a problem like truancy exists. Even those programs that attempt to be more holistic and multi-faceted continue to place a greater emphasis on discipline than on solving many of the problems that lead to truancy. While truancy is often a symptom of a larger set of problems, increasingly communities and school districts appear to be more interested in punishing children for absenteeism rather than understanding the reasons for it in the first place (see also McCluskey, Bynum and Patchin 2004).

Another problem with the punitive approach to truancy is that there are mixed results in terms of its effectiveness (see Baker et al. 2000; McCluskey, Bynum and Patchin 2004; McElvain and Kposowa 2006). It makes little sense to punish students for not coming to school by suspending or expelling them. Moreover, from a labeling perspective something like police intervention and/or confinement could result in a negative label by school officials and further propel that child into additional delinquency. For chronic truants, suspension or other punishments will not likely deter them nor will it likely result in compliance (Lemert 1951). In sum, the increasing role of criminal justice as a mechanism to reduce truancy is consistent with a "get tough" philosophy towards crime and delinquency. However, in the case of status offenders, the crime control model may end up exacerbating the problem or worse, failing to recognize the significance of truancy as a symptom of a set of larger problems.

Causes of Truancy

According to the National School Safety Center, about 5% of students in grades 9–12 skip school because they feel unsafe at school or on their way to or from school. Others miss school because of family health issues and financial demands, substance abuse, or mental health problems. Research shows that some of the most important factors contributing to truancy stem from four areas: school configuration, personal and developmental issues, the student's family situation, and community characteristics (Baker, Sigmon, and Nugent 2001).

School Configuration

According to the National Center for Education Statistics, large school systems in low income, inner-city urban school districts have higher rates of absenteeism and truancy compared to suburban and rural school systems. Research consistently reports high absenteeism rates for urban schools, with approximately eight percent of these students labeled chronically truant (Epstein and Sheldon 2002).

Truancy is also more likely to occur in those schools that have not made attendance a priority in terms of policy, in those settings where there is little or no constructive interaction between teachers and parents, and in those schools with a high percentage of uncertified teachers (Dougherty 1999; Epstein and Sheldon 2002). Truancy is also related to low teacher expectations, high teacher absenteeism, and inconsistency in school discipline (Baker et al. 2001; Strickland 1998).

Personal and Developmental Issues

Typically, the problems of absenteeism and truancy stem from the experience the child has while in the classroom. There is a wealth of research that suggests poor performance causes students to lose interest in school. The result is that they fall behind and begin to avoid class, then stop going to school completely. The response by the school to the lack of attendance is usually punitive, which further alienates the student from the institution (Allen-Meares, Washington and Welsh 2000). The onset of this problem is particularly apparent in middle school. School officials often perceive truancy as a lack of interest in school. Given the limited budgets, teachers and administrators sometimes "write off" students; focusing instead on those that are present and interested. This creates a self-fulfilling prophecy in that once the student begins to fail and gives up, the system does not have mechanisms in place to get them back on track.

Family Issues

There is evidence to indicate that there is an inverse relationship between parental involvement and truancy. When parents participate in their child's education, whether it be monitoring homework, helping to improve their reading ability, or attending PTA meetings, the probability of truancy decreases (Epstein and Sheldon 2002). Parental involvement is also related to social class. Research shows that parents with high socio-economic status (SES) tend to be more involved with teachers and schools as well as being more involved with their child's educational and learning development.

Part of the reason for this is that affluent parents tend to have more resources, time to spend with their children, and they place a high value on education. Youths from single parent homes tend to have higher rates of absenteeism and truancy than youths from two-parent households, which tend to be lower income families (Oman et al. 2002; Klein 1994). One study found that youths who lived in one-parent households had a greater likelihood of skipping school, fighting, using alcohol or tobacco and participating in sexual intercourse (Rohrman 1993). Other studies show that where parenting styles are weak or nonexistent, meaning children are given too much autonomy in decision making and less corrective direction, truancy increases (Oman et al. 2002; Rohrman 1993).

Neighborhood and Community Factors

As was mentioned, social class is an important variable in understanding truancy. Children living in low-income and/or inner-city neighborhoods are more likely than suburban youth to experience acts of violence, maltreatment, neglect and abuse, and receive below average educations. This, in turn, affects student motivation about education in general and attending school in particular.

Related to social class, of course, are the physical conditions of neighborhoods in which children live. The research demonstrates a substantial link between neighborhood context and truancy (see for instance Epstein and Sheldon 2002; Teevan and Dryburgh 2000). Exposure to mental and physical health stressors (e.g. abuse, neglect, domestic violence, family strife) and other signs of disorder (e.g. abandoned buildings and cars, condemned housing, illegal drug markets) are all related to truancy (Wandersman and Nation 1999).

The Costs of Truancy

The costs of truancy are significant: high school dropouts claim more in government funded social services expenditures than high school graduates. For men in particular, dropouts incur more in criminal justice costs. The average dropout costs society more than $800,000 over the course of his or her lifetime. Discounted for the current value of money, that amount is approximately $200,000. A study of the costs and benefits of three truancy reduction programs and three truancy courts operating in Colorado discovered that since one high school dropout costs $200,000, the truancy programs operating in Adams County and the City of Denver, which serve about 85 students a year, each of which cost about $50,000 a year, can operate for four years for the same cost (National Center for School Engagement 2005). Therefore, even if those programs only encourage one out of 300 program participants to graduate from high school, they will yield a positive return on their investment.

The cost/benefits of truancy programs in general are readily self-evident: while cost assessment studies are limited, given their low cost of operation, and the high cost of dropping out, it is likely that all truancy reduction programs pay for themselves many times over.

Strategies That Work to Reduce Truancy

While every state has its own set of laws regarding truancy, and national trends do not always reflect local policy, it is important to note that there is no single cause for truancy. This means there is no single model for each state to follow. However, there is substantial evidence to suggest that the most effective programs are those that can demonstrate an alliance between parents and teachers, systematic monitoring and recording of absenteeism and truancy, a consistent imposition of penalties for repeat offenders, support for intervention programs, and patience with regard to implementing new programs (Teasley 2004).

The evidence also shows that those highly punitive programs that place the problem of truancy on the individual have not curbed truancy rates. Zero tolerance polices have done more to alienate students from school than to improve teaching and learning (Civil Rights Project 2000). The best programs seem to be those that have a "carrot and stick" approach, whereby parents are involved, students are held accountable by both the school district and the courts, who are working collaboratively rather than trying to shift their burden of responsibility.

Court-imposed sanctions beyond school suspension on both the parent and the child and some sort of positive reinforcement to the child is also important. The hard line approach to truancy is that attending school is not something students should be rewarded for, but the realities of the lives of many students is that they need something to say "yes" to rather than being told about the potential negative consequences of their actions.

Proponents of this approach argue that this is not coddling kids, rather it is realizing that simply expecting this generation of children to do what they are supposed to do "or else" is an ineffective way of addressing truancy. Granted, there are some children for whom any help will be limited, however, the more proactive approach is designed to alleviate the problem before it becomes chronic. Positive reinforcement, even for small things like completing a life skills program, which is part of some anti-truancy prevention programs, can have a significant impact on a young person who is deciding which behavioral path to take: conformity, education and success or delinquency, crime, and substance abuse.

Innovative Ways to Combat Truancy

In an effort to address truancy in schools, many states have offered a variety of programs: suspension for missing a certain number of classes, fining the parents for each day the child misses school, and other punitive measures. However, as was mentioned, punishing a child who does not want to come to school with removal from the classroom is an illogical and counterproductive approach. Similarly, fining a parent for the behavior of the child, while clearly providing an incentive to motivate the parent to elicit the cooperation of the child, holds little in the way of real accountability for the one who is failing to show up for school. The data clearly demonstrate that these programs have had very little impact on the problem of truancy. Consequently, many states are beginning to recognize that the best way to get school attendance to improve begins with making the problem of missing school painful to the student. They accomplish this by asking the obvious question: "What do kids want?"

Obtaining a driver's license is a teenager's symbolic sign of maturity, freedom, and a passport to adulthood. Given its social and practical importance for teens, many states have begun using it to improve school attendance. A number of states, including New Jersey, Minnesota, and South Carolina, have implemented programs that stipulate if a student has more than an allotted number of unexcused absences in a year, the student's right to obtain a driver's license is delayed for a fixed period of time, usually six months. In those cases where students miss school but already have their license, it is revoked/suspended for the same period of time. Additionally, some states are currently developing added punishments for repeat offenders (Jones 2005).

Critics contend that states do not possess the authority to revoke a driver's license for a school-related behavior. However, proponents of this approach argue that a driver's license is not a right but a privilege extended to those who demonstrate sufficient maturity, responsibility, and trust—a student who does not attend school demonstrates a lack of all three. There also exists a legal precedent that reinforces the argument that a driver's license is not guaranteed. For instance, many states, such as New Jersey, provide for the suspension of a driver's license if a parent is delinquent in paying their child support awards. A license suspension also occurs when a person fails to appear at a child support hearing or when an arrest warrant is issued for nonpayment of support (Jones 2005).

Another way to decrease truancy is to link welfare assistance to satisfactory school attendance (Wright 2005). Beginning in the late 1980s a number of states began implementing a program that is similar to welfare-to-work initiatives. Linking welfare benefits to school attendance was said by some experts to reinforce the idea supporting the parameters and spirit of the Welfare Reform Act of 1999 (Wright 2005). However, it should be noted that there is a wealth of evidence that suggests truancy is not the primary issue of school absenteeism among welfare recipients: health issues are the major cause of the problem (Fein et al. 1999). Thus, students on welfare are not avoiding school for conventional reasons (e.g. poor performance, laziness). Rather, health conditions or related problems within the family explain why they miss school. Thus, strategies to address truancy for this group should take the somewhat unique circumstances into account for this segment of the truant population.

Other communities, such as Houston, Texas, have implemented volunteer programs, where, in 2005, for example, school officials and community residents visited more than 600 homes to persuade older truants and dropouts to return to school. Many students who had dropped out cited daycare and employment responsibilities as the reason they left school. Many, however, said they simply got into the habit of not showing up for school, particularly if their parents worked during the day (Stover 2005).

Still other communities have turned to technology to reduce truancy. In 1998 The Oakland Unified School District had an absentee rate of between 3,000 and 3,500 students per day, or 15% of the entire student population. At a loss of $19 per student per day, the school district was losing nearly $4 million in attendance revenue each year. This led the district to implement the PhoneMaster 2000 system. This system was developed to increase parents' awareness by calling the home of each student absent two or more periods each day. The system calls the parents or guardians of the children between 7pm and 9pm on school nights. If the parent answers, they enter a PIN number and the system informs them of the absences and allows them to excuse their child by offering an array of choices. The system also establishes an audio text message from each teacher. Parents can access information, such as what was covered in class that day or dates for assignments and tests. The overall objective was to allow parents a more active role in their child's education (Phone-Master Systems 1998).

Boston has a wireless system that allows police and truant officers access to student records. Given that nearly 5% of Boston's 64,000 students are truant for more than five days during the school year, this feature, which can be tied into an officer's cell phone, allows local probation and police officers to sweep "hot spots" with truant officers where they can immediately check court, police, and school records of the teenagers they locate (Trotter 2002).

South Carolina Courts and Truancy

While many states have reestablished the authority of the courts as the main strategy to address truancy, courts in general have been notoriously slow in dealing with truancy cases. For example, in Dallas County, Texas, one study found that truancy cases sat in courts an average of 73 days before a hearing was conducted, with some cases waiting up to 160 days (Capps 2003). Moreover, many families are not intimidated by courts when it comes to acts of truancy (ABA 2001). Thus, even when the case gets to court, parents have a difficult time understanding the seriousness of the problem. Aside from this, the wisdom of putting children in non-secure detention or foster care is often counterproductive because such measures are traumatic for the families, are cost-prohibitive, and often end up taking students out of school (Mogulescu and Segal 2002).

In South Carolina, all children between the ages of 5 and 17 are required to attend a public or private school or an approved home study program unless they graduate from high school before age 17. There are a few exceptions to this rule, such as a child who has graduated from high school or received a GED; a child who completes the 8th grade and is gainfully employed and employment is important to the maintenance of the child's home. A parent or guardian who fails to make their children attend school can be charged with educational neglect (Children's Law Center 2005).

Truancy, as defined by the state, consists of three unexcused absences in a row or five all together during the year. The South Carolina Code of Regulations, R. 43-274, has three categories of truancy. First, a truant is a child who is 6 to 17 years old, who has three consecutive unlawful absences or a total of five unlawful absences. Second, a "habitual" truant is a child who is 12 to 17 years old, who does not comply with the intervention plan developed by the school, the child, and the parents or guardians, and who accumulates two or more additional unlawful absences. Third, a "chronic" truant is a child, 12 to 17 years old, who has been through the school intervention process, has reached the level of habitual truant, has been referred to family court and placed under an order to attend school, and continues to accumulate unlawful absences.

Initially, when the child meets the minimum number of absences, the school is required to meet with the child and the parents to develop some type of plan to prevent future problems with attendance. Failure to compel their children to attend school can result in parents being fined up to fifty dollars for each absence or incarceration for up to 30 days for each absence. Should the child fail to attend school and continue to miss classes, he or she may be brought to Family Court to appear before a judge. If the child continues to miss school and defy the court's mandate, the judge has the authority to find the child guilty of contempt of court and detain the child through the Department of Juvenile Justice for a period of up to 90 days. It is at this point the child is considered a chronic truant and in need of some type of intervention.

Prior to 2005, the nature of truancy in Charleston county was excessively high. There were no truant officers in Charleston and SROs in each school were burdened with other responsibilities and obligations, so they could not keep track of truants. The school district had no intervention plan in place when a child became truant and virtually no referrals to other outside agencies. Essentially, school officials were not paying attention to truancy or were content to have problem students fail to come to school, where they were often a disruptive element. What the school district typically did with truants was to refer them to Family Court for disposition. That way, the responsibility for truants and for truancy in general, fell outside the parameters of the school district (McNamara, 2005).

In response, a Family Court judge, a Solicitor (district attorney), and several other key officials developed a program to address issues relating to truancy and drug offenses. Citing the research that attests to the fact that truancy is a gateway activity to long-term delinquency and crime, as well as recognizing that other agencies should be making truancy a priority, the Barrett Lawrimore Juvenile Drug Court and Accountability Court was created. The program is multi-disciplinary in fighting truancy and educational neglect. It is a collaborative effort between twelve different agencies ranging from the Department of Juvenile Justice, the Charleston County School District, the Department of Mental Health, the Public Defender's Office, and the Charleston County Family Court.

According to internal documents, the program consists of three phases. Initially, once the child is brought before the court, he or she is placed on probation and the parent is placed under a court order to ensure their child(ren) attend school. If the parent and child successfully complete the program, the case is reopened and the charges are dismissed, which means that they are removed from the child's juvenile record.

In Phase I of the program, which lasts for twelve weeks, the student attends a life skills counseling program and their parent(s) or guardian(s) attend a parenting course. These courses are offered two afternoons each week. In addition, the truant and parent appear in court weekly. The parent pays a nominal fee for their counseling program, while the cost of the truant's program is billed to Medicaid. Both the truant and the parent are subject to any drug and alcohol testing ordered by the court. In addition to court appearances and the parenting course, the parent is required to make certain their child attends school each day and enforce a one hour homework session each night. The truant is required to attend school each day with no unexcused absences, skipped classes, or behavior problems. They also participate in any tutoring set up by the court or the school district and maintain satisfactory grades in all courses. The truant's curfew is 7pm as long as they are making satisfactory grades, have no behavior problems, and are following the rules of the program.

If a parent violates the rules, he or she is subject to contempt of court, which carries a sentence of up to one year in jail, a $1,500 fine and/or 300 hours of community service. If the parent does not make sure the child gets to school, he or she can be fined the aforementioned fifty dollars each day the child misses school. In addition, if the court feels that the child's best interests are served by having the parent present with them in school, the parent is required to do so.

If the child skips school or a class, he or she spends each weekend in detention at the Department of Juvenile Justice, which continues until attendance is acceptable to the court. If the child misbehaves while in school, the child is subject to detention, community service, or counseling. Should the parent or child not complete Phase I successfully, they will be assessed by the Department of Mental Health to determine what should be added to the program to make their successful completion the second time around.

For those who have completed Phase I, they are required to appear in court once a month for monitoring. In Phase II, their curfew is raised to 8pm. As long as they remain in good standing and comply with the rules of the program, this phase lasts for twelve weeks. If they begin violating the rules, they return to Phase I and are assessed for additional services. If the participants complete Phase II successfully, their curfew is increased to 9pm and they do not have to appear in court as long as they continue to comply with the stipulations and rules of the program.

It should be noted that as of October 2005, there were 18 children enrolled in the program. This was partly because of the newness of the program, but it was also due to the fact that the Family Court has required the Charleston County school district to implement an effective early intervention program that prevents many children from ending up in court. As a result, the small number was somewhat of a testimony to the effectiveness of this early intervention. The remainder are considered the more difficult children, and the court addresses their issues on a continual basis. An evaluation component is being implemented by the school district in the form of a satisfaction survey of participants. Later, other instruments will be used to determine the overall impact of the program on truancy. What holds promise for this program is the evidence that suggests successful programs are comprised of a few key elements: multi-agency participation, parental involvement, consistent court intervention, and positive reinforcement for participants. It appears that the Accountability Court has all the necessary ingredients to be effective in reducing truancy.

Delaware and Truancy

Delaware operates the nation's only statewide truancy program, which not only emphasizes prevention as a main feature of the program, it also places the responsibility for making sure children attend school on parents. In 1996, Delaware established the Justice of the Peace Court to reduce unexcused absences from school. Modeled after the state drug court, the truancy program has five judges and more than 700 cases per year. One unique feature of the program is that the same judge usually follows each case from the beginning to the end. This results in greater levels of accountability and supervision of truants and their parents. One of the goals of the program, which clearly follows the crime control model discussed earlier, the emphasis is on making parents responsible for their children. To that end, the Court works with various agencies such as the Department of Children, Youth and Their Families to not only create a treatment plan for the family, but to provide services and resources to parents (Corrections Digest 2002).

So successful was this statewide effort that in 2003 The Truancy Court experienced a 29% increase in case filings from 2002. The Truancy Court also appears to be making a difference: 55% of the 739 students with cases closed in 2003 achieved overall compliance with the Truancy Court; 94% of the students achieving full compliance remained in school at the end of the year; 70% of all 2003 students involved with the Truancy Court were still in school at the end of the year; and 66% of all 2002 students involved with the Truancy Court continued to remain in school more than a year later. The Truancy Court was recently honored as the "2003 Program of the Year" by the International Association for Truancy and Dropout Prevention (Justice of the Peace Court Annual Report 2004).

Summary

The problems associated with truancy are significant and their implications have many far reaching consequences. There is substantial evidence that truancy is a gateway activity to an assortment of problems ranging from chronic delinquency, substance abuse, adult crime, teen pregnancy, unemployment, gang behavior, poverty, and dropping out of school. While there are a host of programs designed to reduce and prevent truancy, the most salient features of successful programs are those that involve parents, collaborate and coordinate with the local school district, court intervention for difficult cases, and positive reinforcement for participants along the way. South Carolina's experiment with the Accountability Court holds promise since it includes virtually all of these factors. Moreover, the use of Medicaid to pay for the costs of the program is an innovative idea that relieves the burden of finding financial resources to support it. What remains to be seen is how the program will grow and evolve and the evidence that it is successful in addressing the problems of truancy in Charleston County. Delaware's program serves as a model for states who wish to make truancy a priority as well as addressing the issues surrounding it.

References

Allen-Meares, P. Washington, R. O. and Welsh, B. L. 2000. *Social Work Services in Schools*. Boston: Allyn and Bacon.

Baker, M. L., Signmon, J. N., and Nugent, M. E. 2001.*Truancy Reduction: Keeping Students in School*. Washington, D.C.: U.S. Department of Justice, Office of Juvenile Justice Programs, Office of Juvenile Justice and Delinquency Prevention

Bazemore, G.; Stinchcomb, J. B. and Leip, L. A. 2004. "Scared Straight or Bored Straight? Testing Deterrence Logic in an Evaluation of Police-Led Truancy Intervention." *Justice Quarterly* 21(2):269–300.

Bell, A. J., Rosen, L. A. and Dynlacht, D. 1994. "Truancy Intervention." *The Journal of Research and Development in Education*, 27: 203–211.

Berg, I. 1997. "School Refusal and Truancy." *Archives of Disease in Childhood* 76(2):90–92.

Capps, W. R. 2003. "The New Face of Truancy." *School Administrator*, 60(4):34.

"Case Study: PhoneMaster Systems Reduce Truancy Costs and Headaches." 1998. *T.H.E. Journal* 25(9):68–70.

Catalano, F. R., Arthur, M. W., Hawkins, J. D., Berglund, L., and Olson, J. J. 1998. "Comprehensive Community and School-

Based Interventions to Prevent Antisocial Behavior," in Loeber, R and Farrington, D. eds., *Serious and Violent Juvenile Offenders: Risk Factors and Successful Interventions.* Thousand Oaks, CA: Sage Publications.

Children's Law Center. 2005. *Frequently Asked Questions About Truancy in South Carolina.*

Civil Rights Project Harvard University Conference. 2000. *Opportunities Suspended: The Devastating Consequences of Zero Tolerance and School Discipline Policies.*

Dougherty, J. W. 1999. "Attending to Attendance." *Phi Delta Kappa Fastbacks,* 450:7–49.

Dryfoos, J. G. 1990. *Adolescents at Risk: Prevalence and Prevention.* New York: Oxford University Press.

Epstein, J. L. and Sheldon, S. B. 2002. "Present and Accounted For: Improving Student Attendance Through Family and Community Involvement." *Journal of Educational Research,* 95:308–318.

Fein, D. J., Wang, S. Lee, and E. S. Schofield. 1999. *Do Welfare Recipients' Children Have a School Attendance Problem?* Report prepared for the Delaware Health and Social Services Department, Cambridge, MA: Abt Associates.

Garry, E. M. 1996. *Truancy: First Step to a Lifetime of Problems.* Washington, D.C.: U.S. Department of Justice, Office of Juvenile Justice and Delinquency Prevention.

Heaviside, S., Rowand, C., Williams, C., and Farris, E. 1998. *Violence and Discipline Problems in U. S. Public Schools: 1996–1997.* Washington, D.C.: U. S. Department of Education, Office of Educational Research and Improvement, National Center for Education Statistics.

Huzinga, D. Loeber, R. and Thornberry, T. 1995. *Urban delinquency and Substance Abuse: Initial Findings.* Washington, D.C.: U.S. Department of Justice, Office of Juvenile Justice and Delinquency Prevention.

Jones, L. R. 2005. "Ending School Truancy in One Step." *New Jersey Law Journal,* March 7, 2005.

Justice of the Peace Court Annual Report 2004; accessed at **http://www.courts.delaware.gov** on June 1, 2007).

Kaufman, P., Alt, M. N. and Chapman, C. d. 2001. *Dropout Rates in the United States 2000*. Washington, D.C.: U. S. Department of Education. National Center for Education Statistics.

Kleine, P. A. 1994. *Chronic Absenteeism: A Community Issue.* East Lansing, MI: National Center for Research on Teacher Learning.

McCluskey, C.P., Bynum, T. S., Patchin, J. W. 2004. "Reducing Chronic Absenteeism: An Assessment of an Early Truancy Initiative." *Crime and Delinquency* 50(2):214.

McElvain, J. and Kposowa, A. 2006. "Juvenile Delinquency and Crime Prevention: An Evaluation of a Multi-Agency School Implemented Program." *Journal of California Law Enforcement* 40(4):7–23.

McNamara, R. H. 2005. Personal Communication with Court Official, October 7th.

Mogulescu, S. and Segal, H. J. 2002. Approaches to Truancy Prevention. New York: Vera Institute of Justice, Youth Justice Program. "No Show, No License." *Scholastic Scope* 53(11):21.

Oman, R. F., McLeroy, K. R., Versely, S., Aspy, C. B., Smith, D. W. and Penn, D. A. 2002. "An Adolescent Age Group Approach to Examining Youth Risk Behaviors." *American Journal of Health Promotion*, 16:167–176.

"Prevention is Central in Delaware Program." *Corrections Digest* 33(43):5, October 2002.

Puzzanchera, C., Stahl, A. L., Finnegan, T. A., Tierney, N., Snyder, H. N. 2003. Juvenile Court Statistics 1998. Washington, D.C.: U.S. Department of Justice, Office of Juvenile Justice and Delinquency Prevention.

Rohrman, D. 1993. "Combating Truancy in Our Schools—A Community Effort." *NASSP Bulletin*, 76(549):40–51.

Rubin, H. G. 2004. "NYC Settles Lawsuit Alleging Students Were "Pushed Out." *Education Daily* 37(6):1–2.

Snyder, H. N. and Sickmund, M. 1995. *Juvenile Offenders and Victims: A National Report.* Washington, D.C.: U.S. Department of Justice, Office of Juvenile Justice and Delinquency Prevention

Stover, D. 2005. "New Ways, More Reasons to Fight Truancy." *The Education Digest,* 70(5):48–52.

Strickland, V. P. 1998. *Attendance and Grade Point Average: A Study.* East Lansing, MI: National Center for Research on Teacher Learning.

Teasley, M. L. 2004. "Absenteeism and Truancy: Risk, Protection, and Best PracticeImplications for School Social Workers." *Children and Schools* 26(2):117–129.

Teevan, J. J. and Dryburgh, H. B. 2000. "First Person Accounts and Sociological Explanations of Delinquency." *Canadian Review of Sociology and Anthropology* 37(1):77–93.

Trotter, A. 2002. "Boston Will Use New Cellphones to Call Truants' Bluff." *Education Week,* 21(31):1–3.

U. S. Department of Education. 1993. *Conditions of Education: 1993.* Washington, D.C.: U.S. Department of Education.

Wandersman, A. and Nation, M. 1998. "Urban Neighborhoods and Mental Health: Psychological Contributions to Understanding Toxicity, Resilience, and Interventions." *American Psychologist* 53:647–656.

Wright, J. 2005. "Rethinking Welfare School Attendance Policies." *Social Service Review,* 79(1):2–27.

4

Incorrigibility and Curfew Violations

It's a common lament by parents: their children do not listen or obey them or the rules of their household. Parents with teenagers are especially sensitive to disobedience: the teen years are usually the most difficult ones for a family to overcome. But some parents have acutely difficult and uncontrollable children—these are considered incorrigible or ungovernable.

By definition, incorrigibility consists of juveniles who habitually do not obey their parents. This type of behavior received a lot of attention during the 1970s. With *parens patriae* still operating, many juveniles were incarcerated for incorrigibility. Critics argued that almost all juveniles disobey their parents at some point and such behavior may not always warrant court action. Incarceration for such behavior consequently exposed juveniles to much more severe criminality and sometimes even sexual and physical abuse. In short, juveniles came out of the system worse than when they entered it.

Historical Roots of Incorrigibility

Laws regulating children's behavior and obedience to parents go back to early Roman and Greek cultures. In Europe and early America, children were apprenticed at an early age, which often led to exploitation, beatings, and other forms of abuse. Paradoxically, while some children were loved by their parents, others were ignored; while some children were treated with care, others were disciplined harshly. The indifference towards children during this period in history was evidenced by their high death rate (Bannister, Carter, and Schafer 2001).

During the seventeenth and eighteenth centuries, interest in improving child-rearing practices began. Church and school officials promoted the idea that children were special and fragile, but also corruptible and trying. The church, the family, the community, and the school were to join in fostering their development and controlling misbehaviors. Principles emerged that stressed discipline, modesty, chastity, hard work, and obedience to authority. Such Puritan values were very influential but not universal in the North American colonies. There was an interest in helping the poor who helped themselves, but not in others who had little motivation or did not believe in hard work. This distinction has been seen in most of social policy throughout American history.

As Blau (1992) points out, the *deserving poor* were those individuals who, through no fault of their own, found themselves in impoverished situations. In contrast, the *undeserving poor* were those individuals who had no work ethic, were not interested in a better life, and were generally considered unworthy of societal assistance. This same attitude applied to children. The Massachusetts "stubborn child," used as late as the 1970s, was passed in 1654 when the House of Deputies of the Colony of the Massachusetts Bay in New England determined that children often misbehaved and treated authority figures with little or no respect. The colony provided corporal punishment such as whippings for young offenders.

The Massachusetts Constitution of 1780 authorized the incorporation of these and other early laws into the statutes of the Commonwealth. Over time, simplifying amendments were made, but as late as 1971, the state's Supreme Court upheld the stubborn child statute against a complaint that the statute was so vague and indefinite as to violate constitutional due process requirements (*Commonwealth v. Brother*, Supreme Court of Massachusetts, 270 N.E. 2d 389 (Mass.), 1971).

Numerous social and societal changes, particularly the influence of humanitarianism found in the philosophy of Enlightenment, led to a sense of optimism at helping the less fortunate. Again, the focus was on adults, not children. Wayward youth commonly were held, not helped, in impoverished almshouses and regularly sentenced to jail where they lived side by side with adult inmates. Beginning about 1825, specialized institutions were founded, such as orphan asylums for abandoned children and houses of refuge for runaway, disobedient, or vagrant youth. Later, training schools and reformatories for young offenders were established, but jailing remained common. Accurate data of the official handling of incorrigibility are still difficult to come by, however, an examination of archival data of the offenses recorded for juveniles committed to the Wisconsin State Reform School between 1880–1889 and 1890–1899 found 50% of inmates had been committed for "incorrigibility" (Steinhart 1996).

Incorrigibility and the Juvenile Justice System

As was mentioned, there has been an increasing emphasis on detention and other punitive measures to address the problems relating to delinquents. Unfortunately, status offenders have been grouped into this category, resulting in detention despite the fact that federal law prohibits incarcerating this type of offender. A 2004 report by the Office of Juvenile Justice and Delinquency Prevention, found that an increasing percentage of detained juveniles were being held in locked facilities. Juveniles in residential placement for homicide, robbery, and aggravated assault were the most likely to be held behind locked doors or gates.

As Table 4-1 shows, unlike juveniles held for delinquency offenses, those in residential placement for status offenses were more likely to be confined under "staff-secure" rather than under "locked" arrangements. Seven in ten status offenders were confined under staff-secure arrangements. However, substantial variation existed within the status offense categories. Juveniles held for underage drinking or possession of alcohol were as likely to be held in locked arrangements as in staff-secure arrangements. Among those held for running away, curfew violations, and truancy, the proportions of youth locked in were smaller. Juveniles held for incorrigibility were the least likely to be held under locked security arrangements. Part of the explanation for this difference might be due to the threat of escape as well as con-

Table 4-1.
Facility Security Profile of Status Offenders-All Facilities

	Total	Locked	Staff-secure
Status offense	100%	29%	71%
Underage drinking	100	51	49
Runaway	100	40	60
Curfew Violation	100	40	60
Truancy	100	24	76
Incorrigibility	100	18	82
Other status	100	33	67

Source: Office of Juvenile Justice Delinquency Prevention, 2004.

cerns about the youth's safety. With offenses such as drinking, where the youth might be intoxicated and at risk to themselves and others, perhaps officials are more cautious. Similarly there could be instances in which runaways or even curfew violators may pose a risk to themselves. Whatever the reason, the fact that status offenders are increasingly being held in detention facilities of any kind reflects a perception of youth that warrants more severe treatment.

Curfew Violations

Curfew violations are status offenses because these laws impose restrictions based solely on age. A typical curfew law prohibits youth under the age of 16 or 17 from being in a public place during late evening or nighttime hours. These ordinances vary greatly from location to location and most contain exceptions for children who are accompanied by an adult or are traveling to or from some acceptable activity (Juvenile Justice Digest 2003; Steinhart 1996).

Recent concerns about juvenile violent crime has brought a renewed interest in the use and value of curfews for youth. Curfews have always been viewed as a form of secondary crime prevention, meaning they serve to reduce the motivation of potential offenders to commit crimes. Despite a long history of use in this country, dating back hundreds of years, the public's fear of violent crime has resulted in a regeneration of their use. In the 1990s, a survey of America's largest 200 cities showed that 73% had curfew ordinances. Of those surveyed cities, 21% had curfews for one year or less. National data reported by the FBI found arrests for violation of curfew and loitering laws had increased 14% from1994 to 1995 (Uniform Crime Reports 2000).

More recently, in places like South Bend, Indiana, the police department strictly enforces a teen curfew which prohibits minors from being on the streets after 11pm on weekdays and 1 am on weekends. Fines up to $500 can be assessed against the parents of teens who violate the curfew. While the department is selective in its curfew patrols, its schedule is based on trends in juvenile crime. In 2003, the 15 officers from the Neighborhood Enforcement Services team and Gang Intervention Unit cracked down on unaccompanied teens, allegedly reducing juvenile crime during that summer (Juvenile Justice Digest 2003).

Curfews are controversial, with proponents believing they reduce crime, while opponents say they stigmatize primarily underclass minority youths. However, there remain a number of questions about the efficacy of curfew laws, particularly as they relate to reducing juvenile crime. There does not appear to be sufficient empirical evidence to support the widespread use of curfews, however the public's concerns about the rise of juvenile crime may supersede the validity of this practice (see for instance Bannister, Carter and Schafer 2001; Lersch and Sellers 2000; Juvenile Justice Update 2000). Part of the problem is that evaluations of curfews are typically conducted by agency personnel and the instruments used are flawed. This does not suggest that curfews, by themselves, are ineffective in reducing delinquency; rather it suggests that there is an absence of definitive data that convincingly concludes that curfews work (Bannister, Carter and Schafer 2001). In short, while curfews may make the public feel as though they are doing something significant about juvenile crime, the data simply does not support this conclusion. Rather than addressing the specific problems relating to delinquency, curfew laws allow municipalities to cast a wide net of restrictions on youth under the umbrella of public safety. Not surprisingly, given the popularity of curfews, one of the most frequent crimes for which juveniles are arrested is curfew violation. According to the UCR, there were approximately 140,000 curfew arrests in 2005.

Historical Roots of Curfews

The term "curfew" derives from the French, "couvre feu," to cover the fire, and is associated with public safety regulations requiring, at a given time or upon a signal, such as the ringing of a bell, that fires in homes be "covered or protected for the night" (Ghent 2004). As Rhyne (1943) notes, curfews have existed for more than 1,100 years, dating back to Alfred the Great in England. During this time period, a bell was rung to signal residents of Oxford that they should return to their homes for the night. This same mechanism of social control was used during the reign of William the Conqueror (1066–1087). In general the curfew was designed to prevent Saxons from gathering and causing civil disturbances (Ghent 2004).

The same strategy was employed in the U.S. during slavery in the South. The terminology "curfew" had its origins in the locking of city gates at night and its more recent use is borrowed from the practices which deny freedom of movement to many juveniles (Rhyne 1943).

By the end of the nineteenth century, curfews were fairly common in the U.S., over 3,000 communities had them and their justification is still used today (Harvard Law Review 2005). Those in favor of curfews argue that because of the decline of the traditional family, children were failing to grow into productive members of society. Those opposed to curfews replied that most juvenile crimes occurred in daylight hours and that most children were not criminals. Despite this debate, curfews were quite popular.

Perhaps due to the start of World War I, Prohibition, or the Great Depression, national concern over juvenile curfews were eclipsed by other issues. It was not until World War II that curfews once again became a topic of importance for Americans. This popularity increased significantly when parents were drafted or worked in factories to support the war effort, which left many children inadequately supervised (Ruefle and Reynolds 1996).

Initially, curfews were designed to protect youth from the vice and corrupting influences that were found in many large cities. Curfews also served as a way to prevent crime. As the public and policymakers learned more about status offenses and gateway activities that led to serious forms of delinquency, curfews became a tool to limit contact between juveniles.

In the 1990s, juvenile victimization and crime rates increased dramatically across the country. This led to the resurgence of interest in curfews. Advocates viewed them as a necessary step toward stopping the rising tide of juvenile crime. Politicians and policymakers also felt that curfews represented a tangible way to show they were tough on crime and were holding delinquents accountable for their actions. This perception was underscored by an apparent empirical link between curfews and juvenile crime: in some places where a curfew was imposed, it appeared that the juvenile crime rate decreased. The popularity of curfews, as well as this perception of their effectiveness, is seen in public opinion polls that show adults approve of youth curfews and believe that they are effective in reducing youth crime (Privor and Ruefle 1995).

By 1995, 77% of cities with populations greater than 200,000 had some form of juvenile curfew, 60% of which were either enacted or enhanced after 1990 (McDowell, Loftin, and Weiserma 2000). However, the popularity of curfews was not limited to large cities, in 1995, 73% of cities of more than 100,000 had curfews and by 1997, 80% of communities with populations greater than 30,000 had them. In essence, over the course of a century, America effectively closed the streets to minors at night (Harvard Law Review 2005).

The Debate about Juvenile Curfews

Proponents of Curfews

On one hand, curfews are justified by community residents, activists, and politicians not only as a way to control youth gangs and as a deterrent to delinquency in general, but to protect youth from victimization. Some also argue that curfews send a clear message about what is appropriate behavior for youth in a given community. Related to this is the fact that curfews provide clear boundaries and supervision of youth to those agencies charged with enforcing curfew laws.

Proponents of curfews also believe that such laws give parents an extra tool to keep children safe. The argument is that children who are off the streets at night are less likely to be victims of crime. Advocates argue that curfews can also be a part of a larger outreach program to help at-risk youth. Finally, curfews give the police more resources with which to fight crime in their communities (Aitken 2003).

The belief in curfews is underscored by anecdotal evidence where some communities have had success in reducing juvenile crime. Between 1993 and 1994, for example, the Dallas Police Department reported an 18% decrease in victimization of youth and a 15% decrease in juvenile arrests. According to the National Center for Policy Analysis, which examined the U.S. Conference of Mayors study in 1997, in 26 cities that compiled statistics with curfews, juvenile crime decreased by an average of 21%. However, caution must be used in interpreting the data as some communities only report aggregated trends, not trends relating to a before- and after design of the curfew.

Opponents of Curfews

Essentially there are two arguments against the use of curfews: they are discriminatory and they are ineffective. Perhaps the loudest criticism against curfews relates to the uneven enforcement of curfew laws against minority youth. In San Jose, California, nearly 60% of juveniles detained under the city's curfew law were Latino, which was disproportionate to the size of that segment of the population. Despite the fact that curfews have strong support in minority communities, some fear they are unfairly enforced against racial minorities (Privor 1999). Critics argue that juvenile curfews are little more than contemporary examples of World War II-era ethnic curfews or even analogous to restrictions placed on slaves during the pre Civil War era. Confinement to home is less problematic, critics say, when there is ample room in the house and many things to do, as in affluent homes. Thus, because of social class and economic inequality, minority youth are unfairly punished compared to their more affluent counterparts (Males and Macallair 1998).

Another criticism of curfews is that the evaluations of their effectiveness are methodologically flawed. As a result, while curfews may be interpreted as successful, this may not be the case. Methodologically, virtually all of the studies of curfews fail to construct a control group to make empirical comparisons. Often success is determined only by a decrease in the crime rate in a given community. However, there are a host of factors that contribute to a drop in crime and parceling out the role of the curfew is virtually impossible without some sort of control mechanism. Moreover, care must be used when interpreting overall decreases in crime. While an overall drop in the crime rate may occur shortly after enacting a curfew law, it is important to examine not just the overall crime rate, but the rates of crime for the target population. It makes no sense, for example, to cite a decrease in crime as a result of a curfew law only to discover it was due to a decrease in adult crime (Budd 1999).

There are also questions about the logic involved in curfew laws. There is some evidence, for example, that curfews displace crime into non-curfew hours and that official crime statistics may not be a reliable way to show the relationship between juvenile crime and curfew enforcement. Researchers at the Center on Juvenile and Criminal Justice found that counties that had strict curfews did not see a decrease in youth crime greater than those counties without such curfews. One such example is cited by Budd (1999) where the City of San Diego cited an overall drop in arrests for juvenile crime during the first year of San Diego's curfew enforcement program. The data "proved" that the curfew program was a success. However, the data actually demonstrated that the crime rate during curfew hours remained essentially unchanged (233 arrests in one year vs. 222 a year later) while the crime rate during non-curfew hours dropped dramatically. The implication, of course was that San Diego credited its juvenile curfew program with a decline in crime that occurred almost entirely during the period when the curfew was not in effect. Additional analysis showed that less than 15% of all arrests for violent juvenile crime in

San Diego occurred during curfew hours. This was and continues to be consistent with national data indicating that juvenile crime peaks at 3pm and then again at 6pm, well before curfews take effect. Thus, even if curfews were effective, they would only reach a small percentage of the juvenile crime that is committed in a community (Budd 1999).

The Weight of the Empirical Evidence on Juvenile Curfews

According to a recent study by Adams (2003) while curfews have become a popular strategy to control delinquency, and while public opinion is solidly behind the use of curfews, a review of the research concludes that there is little overall evidence to suggest that curfews prevent crime and victimization. That is, juvenile crime is likely to remain unchanged after implementing a curfew law, particularly over time. In fact, this has been the case for as long as the effectiveness of curfews has been studied. According to Budd (1999), there is no empirical research that demonstrates that curfews have any appreciable effect on rates of juvenile crime. Citing Ruefle and Reynolds's (1995) study, as well as several others, which argue that because most juvenile crime occurs before the hours spanned by the typical curfew (with recent estimates that 50% of juvenile crime occurs between the hours of 3pm and 9pm), the possible impact of a curfew on juvenile crime is negligible.

Budd (1999) also argues that the premise on which juvenile curfews is flawed. Given that the most severe level of punishment is likely to be a misdemeanor summons, curfews do not sufficiently deter youth who would be willing to risk more punitive punishments should they be caught (such as burglary or robbery). Thus, if youth are willing to ignore the potential punishments for committing these acts, certainly the mild punishments meted out for violating their curfew (which is designed to prevent such crimes) is unlikely to be effective. McDowell, Loftin, and Wieserma (2000) analyzed data from 57 cities with populations of 250,000 or more. They found extremely weak support for the relationship between curfews and juvenile crime. While they noted significant reductions in the number of burglary, larceny and simple assault arrests, McDowell argued that the effects of the curfew were minimal.

Another study explored the effectiveness of a curfew in New Orleans, described as the most restrictive in the U.S. at the time. Ultimately the curfew was ineffective in reducing crime and victimization. There was also an increase in victimizations during non-curfew hours after the ordinance took effect. In general, few who study them assert that curfew laws are effective despite anecdotal evidence from agencies and municipalities who demonstrate some impact on juvenile crime (Lersh and Sellers 2000).

Males and Macallair (1998) compared jurisdictions in California that strictly enforced juvenile curfews with those that did not. Based on their analysis, they found that there was "no basis to the belief that curfew laws are an effective way for communities to prevent youth crime and keep young people safe" (p.15).

Other researchers point out that while the objectives related to curfews have value, communities go about implementing them in the wrong way. Dale Blyth, Director of Research and Evaluation of the Search Institute in Minneapolis, MN, says:

> Our research and other research shows that structured time use is clearly related to positive youth development. But taking a regulatory approach isn't the whole answer, we also need to provide kids with constructive opportunities. Instead of just restricting youth behavior, a community might work to develop teen centers in places youth hang out, like malls. The goal should always be to strengthen the developmental asset that will help kids grow up in healthy ways (Search Institute Report 2003).

Even when communities create curfews, the police tend to use them sparingly. As was mentioned, according to the Uniform Crime Reports, there were approximately 140,000 juveniles arrested for curfew or loitering violations in 2005, a slight decrease from the previous year. The reason for this is likely due to the fact that, like all status offenses, the charge is a minor one, will not likely result in any serious changes in behavior of the youth, and requires a good deal of administrative effort on the part of the officer. Thus, the value gained from making a curfew law arrest is minimal and the effort required to do so is high (Seigel, Welsh, and Senna 2005). As a result, officers are less likely to exercise this option when dealing with a youth.

Perhaps the most common way to enforce curfew laws is through a "catch and release" program, whereby the police arrest the youth and return them to the parents. Another model requires parents to retrieve their children at a processing center where counselors discuss the issues surrounding parental control with them and their child. Still another method employs secure detention and formal processing of the youth through the juvenile court. While curfew violations remain a status offense, and while the Juvenile Justice and Delinquency Prevention Act (1975) prohibits the incarceration of these types of offenders, the 1980 amendment allows the court to detain a youth who has committed a status offense for up to 24 hours in some cases.

The Legality of Curfews

Legal experts question the validity of curfew laws. The American Civil Liberties Union has taken a strong stance against juvenile curfews, essentially arguing that they constitute a house arrest of a youth with no due process. However, while no case has come before the U.S. Supreme Court to decide the constitutionality of juvenile curfews, appellate courts have maintained their viability as long as they are carefully described.

As Bilchik (1996) has pointed out, there have been a number of legal issues generated from the use of curfews. These legal challenges focus most often on the 1st, 4th, 5th, 9th, and 14th amendments to the U.S. Constitution. Whereas the most easily identified issues relating to curfews relate to freedom of speech, religion and assembly (1st amendment), protection against unreasonable searches and seizures (which has been interpreted by the Court to include protection against unreasonable stopping and detaining citizens under the 4th amendment) and the right to due process under the law (5th amendment) are also important. More obscure issues are citizen's right to privacy (9th amendment) and the right to travel and deprivation of liberty without due process of law (14th amendment).

Essentially there are three legal arguments to curfew laws. One of the main challenges comes in the form of contesting the infringement on the freedom of minors. However, the courts have consistently upheld the validity of curfews despite the fact that they may create constitutional challenges with regard to freedom and due process.

In *Bykofsky v. Borough of Middletown*, a U.S. District Court upheld a juvenile curfew challenged on the grounds that it violated juveniles' 1st and 14th amendments and encroached upon parents' rights to raise their children, which is embodied in the 9th amendment and in the due process clause of the 14th amendment. The Court ruled that the stipulations of the curfew did not violate juveniles' right to freedom of speech, assembly, or the parents' rights to raise their children as they saw fit. The Court stated, "The parents' constitutionally protected interest … which the ordinance infringes only minimally, is outweighed by the Borough's interest in protecting immature minors …" (*Bykofsky v. Borough of Middletown* 401 F.Supp. 1242 (1975).

In *Johnson v. Opelousas* (147 Wis. 2d 556), the Fifth Circuit Court of Appeals struck down a curfew similar to the one upheld *in Byksofsky* because the curfew provided no exception to minors attending religious or school meetings, going to or from their jobs, or engaging in interstate travel. Similarly in *Waters v. Barry*, The Court ruled, "The right to walk the streets or to meet publicly with one's friends for a noble purpose or for no purpose at all, and to do so whenever one pleases is an integral component of life in a free and ordered society." (*Waters v. Barry* 711 F. Supp.1125 (1989).

In 1993 the Fifth Circuit Court of Appeals ruled in *Qutb v. Straus* 11 F.3d 488, 492 (5th Circuit Court of Appeals) 1993, that Dallas's curfew laws addressed the concerns raised in the Johnson case. The Court ruled that because of its precise restrictions, the curfew ordinance provided a model for other communities to emulate. This curfew ordinance essentially states that unaccompanied minors, those younger than seventeen or eighteen are prohibited from using public spaces at night, usually between 11p.m. and 6 a.m., during the week, and between midnight and 6 a.m. on weekends. Curfews following these guidelines contain exceptions for minors who are on the street due to an emergency, work reasons, interstate travel, attendance of a sponsored event, participation in First Amendment activities, or an errand for a parent.

A second legal challenge has focused on the content of curfew laws. If curfews are considered legal on constitutional grounds, what types of parameters are set on them to prevent abuses? The Court has ruled that a statute is invalid if it is too general and its "… standards result in erratic and arbitrary application based on individual impressions and personal predilections." *(Qutb v. Straus* 11 F.3d 488, 492 , 5th Circuit Court of Appeals 1993).

What this means is that statutes that broadly restrict juveniles when less rigid measures are available may be voided. Therefore when cities and states create curfews, they must meet a litmus test relating not only to the constitutional issues mentioned, but also to ensure the legislation is precise in language and specific in terms of its restrictions.

Since the *Qutb* case, other curfew laws have been challenged, which have clouded many of the issues thought to be settled. For instance, in *Nunez v. San Diego*, (114 F. 3d 935, 949, 9th Circuit Court of Appeals 1997), the Ninth Circuit Court of Appeals struck down San Diego's juvenile curfew stating that the curfew violated not only the equal protection clause of the constitution but also First Amendment protections. Although San Diego had "established some nexus between the curfew and its compelling interest of reducing juvenile crime and victimization," the City's failure to adopt the *Qutb's* First Amendment exceptions showed that it was not sufficiently narrow. In *Hutchins v. District of Columbia*, (188 F. 3d 531, 546, D.C. Circuit Court of Appeals) the D.C. Circuit Court upheld the District's curfew, which is identical to the one in Dallas. The Court ruled "juveniles do not have a fundamental right to be on the streets at night without adult supervision."

In *Ramos v. Town of Vernon*, (353 F. 3d 171, 183 2nd Circuit Court of Appeals 2003), the Second Circuit Court ruled that communities must rely on more empirical analysis and "careful study of the problem" rather than on stereotypical assumptions about young people." The town had not conducted a thorough and empirical study of the problem before creating its curfew law and as a result, it failed to meet the scrutiny test. In *Hodgkins v. Peterson*, (355 F. 3d 1048, 7th Circuit Court of Appeals 2004), the Seventh Circuit Court found that Indianapolis's curfew violated the youth's First Amendment protection. Although the curfew pursued significant governmental purpose and had a First Amendment exception, the Court held that the ordinance was not narrowly tailored and failed to allow alternative channels for expression." The court ruled that a "curfew that specified that a law enforcement official must look into whether an affirmative defense applies before making an arrest could pass muster, but Indianapolis's did not."

Part of the problem with some of these rulings relates to the collection of sufficient "data" to justify the enactment of curfews. In some cases, the court ruled that a town acted responsibly in collecting facts and using them as a basis for the ordinance. However, in other cases, courts have taken a narrow view of what was collected and deemed it insufficient as a basis to create the juvenile curfew ordinance.

A third consideration for legislation surrounding juvenile curfews relates to the JJDP Act of 1974, which addresses the deinstitutionalization of status offenders. Recall that this legislation prohibits agencies from detaining status offenders in a secure facility. The only exceptions to this are if the youth is detained for a brief period, not to exceed 24 hours exclusive of weekends and holidays, that provide time for intervention by the juvenile court. The statute also makes exceptions that allow the detention if the offender violates a valid court order or commits a felony. With these restrictions in mind, cities creating curfew laws must establish comprehensive, community-based programs that allow officers to bring curfew violators for temporary detention pending their release to parents or some other disposition.

The rationale for curfews, of course, is to reduce late night juvenile crime and to protect juveniles from being victimized. However, philosophical justifications do not stand the test of legal scrutiny. Law enforcement and community groups who are instrumental in getting curfew legislation passed must present a compelling argument for a particular curfew and when it is needed. This is part of the comprehensive, community-based strategy mentioned earlier. This is accomplished by collecting statistical data on juvenile crime and victimization prior to passing a curfew law. While not a guarantee to stop juvenile crime and victimization, should enough evidence exist to justify such a strategy, it is likely that the courts will uphold its legality.

As part of a comprehensive approach to constructing a curfew law, many of the model programs used in cities around the country typically have one or more of the following components:

- The creation of a curfew center or use of churches or recreation centers to receive juveniles who have been arrested by the police for a curfew violation.
- Staffing of curfew centers with community volunteers and representatives of various social service agencies. This provides an opportunity to address the core issues surrounding the violation rather than simply treating the symptom.
- Referrals to counseling class or service providers for both the parents and the children to address the issues stemming from the violation.
- Some mechanism in place for recidivism including fines, community service, or mandated counseling.
- Recreation and job training programs (Office of Juvenile Justice Delinquency Prevention 2006).

The goal of these types of programs is to remove the punitive dimension of curfew violations and to address the core issues that result in delinquency and/or victimization.

Parental Responsibility and Curfews

What role do parents have in holding their children accountable? In one of the most noted cases concerning parental responsibility, Smolowe (1996) describes the case of the Provenzino family, who discovered that their small home town in Michigan had a law holding parents criminally responsible for the behavior of their children. The Provenzinos had a 16-year-old son Alex, who had been arrested several times and had even attacked his parents, was again arrested for a minor crime. The Provenzinos had recently released their son from a treatment facility for violent juvenile offenders. In response to the son's recent arrest, a district attorney filed charges against the parents. It took a jury only fifteen minutes to convict the Provenzinos of violating the reasonable control over their son. They were fined $300 and ordered to pay an additional $1,000 in court fees.

This case was symbolic of a national trend to address the problems of delinquency as well as parental accountability. Many of these laws force parents into the lives of their children by holding them civilly and criminally liable for their children's actions. Penalties include financial responsibility for restitution payments and court costs as well as financial responsibility for treatment and detention. Parents are also held criminally liable for negligence in their supervision of children. While the laws are popular because they give the appearance of "getting tough" on crime, little evidence exists that such laws have been effective in brought the issue of parental responsibility and accountability for their children to the national level (Smolowe 1996).

Summary

Incorrigibility, sometimes referred to as ungovernability, is the result of parents being unable to control their children. While incarceration was a popular strategy in the 1970s, since then detaining youth for refusing to obey their parents has declined. While the topic has not generated a great deal of scholarly attention, it remains a status offense and is recorded in official statistics. Historically children were not considered legally viable and their treatment by parents or the justice system was not given high priority. However, during the 1970s and 1980s, greater attention was given to the humanitarian treatment of juveniles in general and ungovernable children in particular.

The increase in the use of juvenile curfews is consistent with an overall "get tough" on juvenile crime approach. In general, it appears that the question is not whether juvenile curfews are constitutional, rather it is what type of curfews are constitutional. Clearly curfews are widespread and are given a lot of support in communities around the country. Additionally, despite the empirical evidence that suggests they are less effective, more costly, and time consuming than other potential strategies, because public opinion is so strongly in favor of them, it is unlikely that policymakers and politicians will sway them to some other solution. Although the constitutionality of juvenile curfews has been decided, and while the process of constructing a curfew has become more precise, with detailed guidelines offered to communities around the country as to how to craft such legislation, there remain a number of constitutional issues to be resolved. As evidenced by the cases cited above, the issues and problems surrounding the individual rights and freedoms of juveniles becomes a pivot point on which this discussion evolves. Clearly there remain questions about the efficacy of curfews, which would lead one to wonder why the constitutional issues are even being discussed. However, to date, a clearly defined set of criteria exists about how to create a curfew law, but the quality of the data and the analysis conducted to justify it remains ambiguous. In the end, the value of curfews lies in their ability to give police officers more options when interacting with youth on the street. While it may not have an overall effect on juvenile crime for a number of reasons, perhaps its real value lies in the flexibility it offers officers to prevent a youth from becoming more formally involved in the juvenile justice system.

References

Adams, K. 2003. "The Effectiveness of Juvenile Curfews at Crime Prevention." *The Annals of the American Academy of Political and Social Science*, 587(1): 136–159.

Aitken, M. 2003. *Community Curfews for Youth: Punitive or Positive?* Ann Arbor, MI: The Search Institute.

ACLU Challenges San Diego's Curfew Law; Lawsuit Filed in Federal Court on Behalf of Teenagers, Parents, Press Release by American Civil Liberties Union, March 15,   1995.

Bannister, A. J.; Carter, D.L. and Schafer J. 2001. "A National Police Sure on the Use of Juvenile Curfews." *Journal of Criminal Justice* 29(3):23–240.

Bilchik, S. 1996. *Curfew: An Answer to Juvenile Delinquency and Victimization?* Washington, DC: Office of Juvenile Justice and Delinquency Prevention.

Blau, J. 1992. *The Visible Poor*. New York: Oxford University Press. "Cities with Curfews Trying to Meet Constitutional Test." *Washington Post*, Dec. 26, 1995.

Budd, J.1999. *Juvenile Curfews: The Rights of Minors vs. the Rhetoric of Public Safety*. Washington, DC: American Bar Association.

Davidson, H. 1996. "No Consequences—Re-examining Parental Responsibility Laws." *Stanford Law and Policy Review* 7, 23–25.

Geis, G and Binder, A. 1991. "Sins of Their Children: Parental Responsibility for   Juvenile Delinquency." 5 *Notre Dame Journal of Legal. Ethics & Public Policy* 307.

Ghant, J. 2004. Annotation, *Validity and Construction of Curfew Statute, Ordinance or Proclamation,* 59 A.L.R. 3d 321 (2004).

Henry, T. 1995. "Curfews Attempt to Curb Teen Crime." *USA Today,* Apr. 5th.

"Juvenile Curfews and the Major Confusion over Minor Rights."*Harvard Law Review,* 2005, vol. 118:2400–2421.

Juvenile Justice Digest. 2003. "Indiana Uses Curfews to Cut Summer Crime." 31(15):3, August 18th.

Juvenile Justice Update. 2000. "New Research Fails to Support Effectiveness of Youth Curfew Laws." 6(3): 1, June/July.

Lersch, K. M. and Sellers, C. S. 2000. "A Comparison of Curfew and Noncurfew Violators Using a Self-Report Delinquency Survey." *American Journal of Criminal Justice* 24(2):259–270.

Males, M. A. and Macallair, D. 1998. *The Impact of Juvenile Curfew Laws in California.* San Francisco, CA: Justice Policy Institute.

McDowell, D.; Loftin, C., and Weirsema, B. 2000. "The Effectiveness of Juvenile Curfews on Crime Prevention." *Crime and Delinquency* 46:76–91.

Pennsylvania Legislator's Municipal Deskbook, Third Edition (2006).

Perry, T. 1995. "Teen Curfew in San Diego Upheld." *L.A. Times,* Dec. 19th.

Privor, B. 1999. "Dusk Till Dawn: Children's Rights and the Effectiveness of Juvenile Curfew Ordinances." *Boston University Law Review* 79, pp.415–489.

Rhyne, C. 1943. *Municipal Curfew for Minors: Model Ordinance Annotated.* Washington, D.C.: National Institute of Municipal Law Officers.

Ruefle, W. & Reynolds, K. M. 1995. "Curfews and Delinquency in Major American Cities." *Crime & Delinquency* 41, 347–358.

Senna, L. and Seigel, L. J. 2005. *Delinquency.* Upper Saddle River, NJ: Prentice Hall.

Shepherd, R. E. 1997. "The Proliferation of Juvenile Curfews." *Criminal Justice Magazine,* 12(1), Spring.

Smolowe, J. 1996. "*Parenting on Trial.*" Time, May 20, 1996, p.50.

Steinhart, D. J. 1996. "Status Offenses." *The Juvenile Court* 6(3), Winter.

U.S. Department of Justice, Office of Juvenile Justice and Delinquency Prevention 1996. *Juvenile Justice Bulletin, Curfew: An Answer to Juvenile Delinquency and Victimization.* Washington, DC: U.S. Government Printing Office.

5

Underage Drinking

When children ask their parents for a sip of wine or beer, it is sometimes seen as cute, particularly if the child is a toddler. In older children, parents often use the request to drink as instructional—to teach their children about alcohol. When teens start drinking, parents often use the experience as an opportunity to provide a lesson in judgment, responsibility, and choices. When teens enter college, parents sometimes think that drinking will be a normal part of the college experience. Few parents ever think of these behaviors as necessarily problematic. While some might agree these behaviors could, at an extreme, present problems for teens, few actually think it begins early and remains a feature of young life. However, underage drinking is actually one of the most significant social problems in the U.S.

According to the latest figures, specifically the 2005 National Drug Use and Health Survey (NDUHS), about 11 million persons aged 12 to 20 reported drinking alcohol in the past month. Approximately 7 million were binge drinkers, and 2.3 million were heavy drinkers. The NDUHS defines binge drinking as having five or more drinks on the same occasion: either at the same time or within a couple of hours of each other on at least one day in the past 30 days. Current use is defined as having at least one drink in the past 30 days while heavy drinking consists of someone who has had five or more drinks on the same occasion on each of five or more days in the past 30.

Underage drinkers do not vary much by gender, slightly more males than females reported current alcohol use (29% vs. 28%, respectively), whereas males are more likely to engage in binge drinking (21% vs. 16%) and heavy drinking (8% vs. 4%). With regard to race and ethnicity, past month alcohol use rates for underage drinkers was highest among Whites, at almost 33%. About 26% of Hispanics, 22% of both Native Americans and African Americans, and 16% of Asian Americans reported drinking within the past month. Whites were also most likely to report binge drinking (22%), followed by Native Americans and Hispanics (18% each). Asians and African Americans were the least likely to report binge drinking (7% and 9% respectively). The data suggest that underage drinking is a serious and significant problem for teens. In fact, in 2007, the Surgeon General called underage drinking an "epidemic" and urged parents to recognize the problem it presents to all Americans. Citing its psychological and physical threats, Kenneth Moritsugu, M.D., M.P.H., the acting Surgeon General, issued a National Call to Action to stop underage drinking and to keep others from starting. He states: "Alcohol remains the most heavily abused substance by America's youth. This Call to Action is attempting to change the culture and attitudes toward drinking in America. We can no longer ignore what alcohol is doing to our children" (U.S. Department of Health and Human Services 2007).

Evidence of the significance of underage drinking is also seen in crime statistics. Arrests for liquor law violations are one of the highest of all categories of status offenses. Moreover, liquor law violations are the most likely of all status offenses to be adjudicated. In 2005, the Uniform Crime Reports (UCR) noted 392,438 arrests for liquor law violations, 86,328 of which were those under the age of 18.

The alarming findings by the 2005 Drug Use and Health study are underscored by other surveys on underage drinking. A 2002 study by the National Center on Substance Abuse at Columbia University (CASA), entitled *Teen Tipplers: America's Underage Drinking Epidemic,* found that alcohol is the biggest drug problem among children and young adults. CASA estimates that the annual costs of alcohol use and abuse are approximately $184.6 billion. Approximately 30% of those costs, nearly $53 billion, is related to underage drinking. The costs are seen in alcohol-related traffic accidents, violent crime, injuries, accidental deaths, suicide attempts, fetal alcohol syndrome, and treatment for alcohol abuse.

According to the CASA study, each year over three million teens between the ages of 12 and 17 take a drink of alcohol for the first time. Despite many programs to address the War on Drugs, most high school students are touched by alcohol far more extensively than any other type of drug. By their senior year in high school, nearly 81% of teens have tried alcohol. This figure exceeds the percentage of seniors who have smoked cigarettes (70%) or those who have used marijuana (47%). In contrast, only about 29% of high school seniors have used some other illegal drug (CASA 2002). Thus, despite the fear associated with drugs like crack, crank, heroin, marijuana and other illicit drugs, and despite the many efforts to educate youth on the dangers of using them (e.g. DARE), alcohol presents the biggest threat to American teens.

Underage drinking is not simply a high school phenomenon. While more teens drink as they get older, many have their first alcoholic drink before age 13, which can lead to an increased risk of developing a problem with alcohol. Age matters: about one in five kids who begin drinking before age 21 report problems with alcohol compared to only about 7% of those who waited until majority age to start drinking. Early drinkers are also more likely to binge drink. One study found that while fewer underage students were using alcohol than in the past, those who did drink tended to do so to excess (Wechsler et al. 2000). In 2002, 21.1% of ninth graders, 32.2% of tenth graders, 34% of eleventh graders and 41.6% of twelfth graders report binge drinking in the past 30 days. In total, almost a third, more than five million high school students, binge drink (CASA 2002).

Early alcohol use may have long-lasting consequences. People who begin drinking before age 15 are four times more likely to develop alcohol dependence at some time in their lives compared with those who have their first drink at age 20 or older (Grant and Dawson 1997). Young people who begin drinking before the age of 21 are more than twice as likely to develop alcohol-related problems and individuals who begin drinking before age 15 are four times more likely to become alcohol dependent than those who do not drink before age 21(CASA 2002).One study found that teens who are diagnosed with an alcohol problem during high school are more likely to have drinking problems at age 24 (Rohde et al. 2001).

The real problem with using alcohol at an early age, even if it is to simply experiment, is that most who try it do not stop. Wechsler et al. (2000) found that 90% of students who have ever tried alcohol are still drinking in the twelfth grade. Students who engage in regular alcohol use as teens are at the greatest risk for becoming binge drinkers in college. Research has shown that students who enter college as nondrinkers will likely remain that way through the first two years of college. High school students who drink alcohol more than 10 times in a month are likely to drink in their freshman year of college (Kluger 2001). Preventing student alcohol use and abuse during the early teen years may prove to be the most effective way of reducing the high rates of alcohol use and binge drinking in college. What is not clear, however, is whether starting to drink at an early age actually causes alcoholism or whether it simply indicates an existing vulnerability to alcohol use disorders (Dawson 2000). Some evidence indicates that genetic factors may contribute to the relationship between early drinking and subsequent alcoholism (Brown and D'Amico 2001; Deas and Thomas 2002).

The Role of the Media in Underage Drinking

Another report by CASA revealed that underage drinkers consume about 20% of all the alcohol consumed in the United States, spending $22.5 billion of the $116.2 billion spent on beer, wine and liquor (Center for Disease Control 2000). The major portion of the alcohol consumed by underage drinkers is beer. CASA estimates that $17.2 billion was attributable to beer, $4.3 billion to distilled spirits and $1.0 billion to wine (CASA 2002). Clearly underage drinkers represent a significant portion of the alcohol industry's customer base.

Consequently, the alcohol industry spends billions of dollars each year on advertising, which includes sponsorship of events, Internet advertising, and product placements in movies and TV shows (Scheir et al. 2000). Image advertising, which markets a persona or an image rather than the quality of a product, is aggressively used by the alcohol industry. Several studies suggest that animation and rock music commonly used in beer advertising campaigns have wide appeal among children and young teens. Children are more familiar with the Budweiser characters in commercials than with virtually any other animated figure, including such high profile characters as Smokey the Bear, the Mighty Morphin' Power Rangers, and Kellogg's Frosted Flakes' Tony the Tiger. The implication of this is that the more they identify with the character, the more likely they will choose to drink (Hill et al. 2000).

Johnson and Johnson (1997) found, in a series of studies in New Zealand, that positive attitudes about alcohol advertisements were related to increased adolescent drinking and intentions to drink. In addition, adolescent males who could remember alcohol advertisements at age 15 consumed more alcohol at age 18. What is particularly compelling about this body of work is that alcohol advertising in New Zealand is subject to much more stringent regulations than in the U.S., yet the relationship between advertising and intentions to drink remains significant (see also Richter and Richter 2000).

Experts tend to agree that advertising exerts an influence on teen drinking patterns, but more research is needed to determine the precise relationship between alcohol advertising and underage drinking. The need for such research is particularly important if one considers that beer, the most extensively advertised alcoholic beverage, is also the least expensive, the most widely available, and the top choice of underage drinkers (Richter and Richter 2000).

Relatively recent additions to the product line of the alcohol industry is a new group of sweet-tasting alcoholic beverages, known as "malternatives" or "alcopops" (e.g., Mike's Hard Lemonade, Tequiza, Smirnoff Ice, Skyy Blue). These beverages are sweet, fruit-flavored, malt-based drinks that come in colorful packaging. Most alcopop beverages have approximately five to seven percent alcohol by volume, a level that is comparable to beer (Alcohol Foundation 2004; Menkengas et al. 1998).

Given the significance of advertising and its important role in underage drinking, consumer, parent, religious, health and prevention organizations have stepped up efforts in the past 20 years to reform the advertising of alcoholic beverages. Such efforts resulted in Congressional hearings, government policy statements, and some efforts by the alcohol, advertising and broadcast industries to promote responsible drinking through public service announcements and other program activities (Biederman et al. 2000).

Positive images of alcohol use are not just projected by alcohol advertisers; there also is a significant presence of alcohol messages in movies and on prime-time television shows (CASA 2002). An analysis of 81 G-rated animated films found that nearly half showed characters using or abusing alcohol or tobacco, but that a significant proportion do not portray the long-term consequences of tobacco and alcohol use. In 34% of the movies, alcohol use was associated with wealth or luxury. In 19%, alcohol use was associated with sexual activity. Alcohol use on television shows is often depicted without adverse consequences or in association with humor, wealth, status, and professionalism (Fletcher and Steffins 1999).

Clearly the role of the media is an important consideration in the incidence of underage drinking. As more advertisers target youth as potential customers, even though it would be illegal for them to consume their products, the end result will likely be an increase in underage drinking.

A Key Element to Underage Drinking: Parental Involvement

While there are a host of factors relating to underage drinking, including individual traits, boredom, the need to fit in with others, easy accessibility of alcohol, a youth's ability to cope with stress, peer group influences, academic failure, and many others, the research consistently shows the role of the family as a key element in understanding alcohol use among teens (National Drug Use and Health Survey 2005; CASA 2002; Richter and Richter 2001). Additionally, the more integrated the child is into his or her community and school, the less likely they are to use alcohol (Beiderman et al. 2000).

There are two dimensions to the role of the family and underage drinking. While a family history of alcoholism is a strong risk factor for underage alcohol use, there is also consideration given to family dynamics and the household environment that can result in teens abusing alcohol. With regard to biological factors, studies of adopted children and twins who have grown up in different environments have established that genetic factors play a role in the transmission of alcohol use from parent to child. Adopted children with alcohol-dependent biological parents are at least twice as likely as other adopted children to become alcoholics (CASA 2002). Children of alcoholics are at greater risk for alcohol problems; they tend to initiate alcohol use earlier and engage in problem drinking at a younger age. Children of alcoholics are four times more likely to become alcoholics or alcohol dependent (Wuethrich 2001).

Environmentally, perhaps the most important influence for teen alcohol use is whether or not parents use it. Children who grow up in families with permissive norms on alcohol use or whose parents model drinking as a way to relax or cope with problems are at greater risk for becoming underage drinkers. Some of these findings are linked to the relationship children have with their parents. Having a good or excellent relationship with parents dramatically decreases a teen's risk factor for substance abuse.

According to a National Survey of American Attitudes on Substance Abuse, teens who had a good relationship with either parent had an average 25% lower risk score for substance abuse than the average teen. Those with excellent relationships with both parents had risk scores that were 40% lower. This study also showed that teens with parents who are engaged in their children's lives, supervise their teenagers and impose rules and standards of behavior, are four times less likely to engage in substance abuse than teens whose parents are less involved in their lives (CASA 2001).

In contrast, children left alone to take care of themselves for extended periods of time are almost four times more likely to report having gotten drunk in the last month than other teens. Children of divorced parents also tend to report significantly greater levels of alcohol use than do children from intact families. One study found that 54% of children of divorced parents use alcohol compared to 36% of children of parents who had never divorced. However, research suggests that children often are better able to avoid substance abuse when in a nurturing single parent home than when in a dysfunctional intact one (CASA 2002).

Related to the relationship as well as accountability by parents is the amount of time spent with children. In 2006, CASA issued a report chronicling the relationship between teens and parents as well as the relationship between spending family time together and subsequent underage drinking. The report stated that teens who have infrequent family dinners (two or fewer per week) are twice as likely to smoke daily and get drunk monthly compared to teens who have frequent family dinners (at least five per week). This study was the first time researchers examined the relationship between a teen's current tobacco and alcohol use and family dinners.

The report also reveals that, compared to teens who have five or more family dinners per week, those who have two or fewer are more than twice as likely to have tried cigarettes; more likely to have tried alcohol; were twice as likely to have tried marijuana; and more than twice as likely to say future drug use is very or somewhat likely (CASA 2006).

The Impact of Underage Alcohol Use

What are the implications of alcohol use, particularly for teens? There are a host of physical and emotional issues associated with underage drinking. For instance, according to the National Center for Health Statistics, alcohol is related to the three leading causes of death among teens ages 12 to 18: accidents (including motor vehicle traffic fatalities and drowning), homicide, and suicide Underage drinking is also associated with teen pregnancy and has been linked to poor educational achievement, delinquency, and drug abuse.

Academic Achievement

Students who abuse alcohol are less likely to do well in school and to show a commitment to schooling. Heavy and binge drinkers between the ages of 12 and 17 have been found to be far more likely than nondrinkers to say that their school work is poor, and four to five times more likely to say that they cut classes or skip school. Students at high risk for alcohol abuse are also at risk for repeating a grade, being absent, or suspended from school. High school students who use alcohol or other substances are five times more likely to drop out of school than nonusers (Greenblatt 2000).

Physical Health Issues

Young drinkers run the risk of developing numerous health problems due to alcohol use, such as coronary heart disease, stroke, liver cirrhosis and various forms of cancer. Alcohol abuse is also related to bulimia and anorexia nervosa, as well as with depression and anxiety disorders, particularly among girls. Research suggests that approximately 23% percent of women with bulimia and 6% of those with anorexia have alcohol abuse and/or dependence.

Sexual Behavior

Alcohol use is also closely related to teen sexual activity. Teens who drink are more likely than teens who do not drink to have sex, to have sexual intercourse at an earlier age, and to have more partners. About 5.6 million 15- to 24-year olds report having unprotected sex because they were drinking or using drugs at the time. Perhaps more importantly, while the majority of high school age drinkers and drug users report using condoms, there still exists a large percentage of teens who are at risk for HIV, other sexually transmitted disease, and pregnancy. One study found that 49% of sexually active teens said they were more likely to have sex if they had been drinking and 17% of the sexually active teens said that they were less likely to use a condom when they had been drinking (CASA 2002).

Psychological Effects

The available research indicates that approximately 35% of individuals with a mood disorder and almost half of those with anxiety disorders are alcohol dependent. What is not clear is the causal ordering of these two problems. In some cases, mental disorders occurred after the discovery of alcohol abuse while in other cases, it was a consequence of the disorder (National Institute on Alcohol Abuse and Addiction 2000).

Suicide is also a problem for teen drinkers. While suicide is the third leading cause of death for young people ages 15- to 24-years old, alcohol use is a significant risk factor for suicide attempts. Alcohol is estimated to be involved in about 10% of teen suicides. In one study of suicide among adolescents, 70% of young people who attempted suicide frequently used alcohol and/or other drugs (National Institute on Alcohol Abuse and Addiction 2000).

Additionally, adolescent heavy drinkers and binge drinkers are more than twice as likely as nondrinkers to say they contemplate suicide (Pacific Institute of Research and Evaluation 2000). The estimated national cost of alcohol-related adolescent suicide is $1.5 billion annually. Alcohol may be related to suicide in several ways. For example, drinking may reduce inhibitions and impair the judgment of someone who is contemplating suicide, making suicide attempts more likely (Greenblatt 2000).

Auto Accidents

Alcohol-related motor vehicle fatality rates are nearly twice as great for those between the ages of 18–20 compared to those over age 21. In an effort to reduce traffic fatalities associated with alcohol consumption, the National Minimum Drinking Age Act of 1984 required all states to raise the age at which individuals can purchase and publicly possess alcohol to 21. Failure to comply with the act resulted in states losing federal highway funds under the Federal Highway Aid Act. By 1987, all states had complied with the 21 minimum drinking age law (National Highway Traffic Safety Administration 2000).

In 2005, 33% of students report riding in a car at least once during the past 30 days with a driver who had been drinking and 13% of students report that they had driven a vehicle at least once while under the influence of alcohol (National Drug Use and Health Survey 2005). Male students are twice as likely as female students to have driven after drinking alcohol. About 16% of binge drinkers and about a third of heavy drinkers said that they drive while under the influence. Another study of young drivers found that only 15% of those surveyed reported using a sober designated driver when drinking (Greenblatt 2000; National Highway Traffic Safety Administration 2002).

The minimum drinking age law, the influence of such groups as Mothers Against Drunk Driving (MADD) and Students Against Drunk Driving (SADD), as well as a reduction of the legal blood alcohol limit (BAC) for driving while intoxicated from 0.10 to 0.08 have been part of the explanation for the reduction of traffic fatalities. However, the fact that a third of students are in vehicles with someone drinking suggests that there is still work to be done with regard to changing attitudes about driving while impaired. While clearly there is room for optimism, that nearly one in five students drove at some point while intoxicated suggests more needs to be done to curb underage drinking.

Legal Variability in Underage Drinking Laws

In a 2003 report on the legal implications of underage drinking, the Pacific Institute for Research and Evaluation evaluated laws relating to underage drinking. Included in this study were attempted purchases of alcohol by minors; possession of alcohol by minors; consumption of alcohol by minors; use of false identification cards; and adults who furnish alcohol to minors. The analyses showed that there were considerable differences in the ways states regulate the sale and consumption of alcohol in the United States. For instance, four states prohibited the purchase of alcohol by a minor only if the youth made a false statement or representation of age in order to purchase the alcohol. Ten states allowed minors to possess alcohol in any private location, including a private residence or venue, and three states did not prohibit the furnishing of alcohol to intoxicated individuals.

This study reveals the importance of the relationship between laws that address underage consumption, drinking, and intoxication—the way a particular law exempts some underage drinkers can negate the law's intended effect. Research is needed to assess the impact of these laws and the variations across jurisdictions. This report provided an important step in assessing these state laws (Pacific Institute for Research and Evaluation 2003).

Prevention and Treatment of Underage Drinking

It should be noted that preventing and addressing underage drinking require different screening, assessment, and treatment approaches than those used for adults. Many research-based interventions target the teen's relevant behavior, such as his or her ability to react appropriately to peer pressure, as well as his or her knowledge, attitudes, and intentions regarding alcohol use (Komro and Toomey 2002). Positive beliefs about alcohol's effects and the social acceptability of drinking encourage the adolescent to begin and continue drinking. However, youth often overestimate how much their peers drink and how positive their peers' attitudes are toward drinking. Consequently, most prevention programs include social efforts to address many teens' misconceptions about alcohol use (Baer 2002).

In 2004, the U.S. Department of Justice's Office of Community Oriented Policing Services (COPS) issued a report on underage drinking. Within that report were several strategies designed to assist communities to minimize the impact of underage drinking. Drawing from the available research on evaluations of programs around the country, these strategies represent a number of "best practices" which provide insight into solutions to underage drinking. The strategies are presented at two levels: global community efforts, such as large scale attempts to reduce alcohol consumption in a given community, and micro level efforts designed to assist law enforcement agencies, community groups, and parents to reduce the incidence of underage drinking.

Macro-Level Community Efforts

Reducing the Community's Overall Alcohol Consumption

Any effort to reduce a community's overall drinking pattern has the potential to reduce underage drinking as well. Changing the norms about alcohol's role in the community can affect young people as well as those who can legally drink. Specific responses could include discouraging price discounts on alcohol, restricting the hours or days retailers can sell alcohol, or limiting the number of community alcohol outlets. Additionally, all states have laws governing minors' purchase and possession of alcohol. However, the specifics of the laws vary widely, and their usefulness in constructing responses can be limited by unusual wording or loopholes. The COPS report offers insight into how to clarify these laws to make them more effective.

Awareness Enhancement Programs

Some interventions use a harm-reduction approach. In other words, they attempt to reduce how much or how often young people drink, rather than try to prevent underage drinking altogether. For example, many universities have developed a wide variety of visual aids to correct students' misperceptions of typical drinking behavior among their peers. Given that many youth drink because they think "everyone else is doing it," these programs attempt to provide accurate information on the typical amount of alcohol consumed and the proportion of peers who drink heavily.

Informing underage drinkers that their drinking adversely affects their peers, and that their peers are no longer willing to tolerate it, can encourage young people to reduce their alcohol use. While there is research to substantiate the effectiveness of social norms marketing programs, other studies cast doubt on their effectiveness. For example, Wechsler et al. (2003), compared student drinking patterns at colleges that employed social-norms marketing programs and those that did not. Over a three year period, no decreases in various measures of alcohol use were evident at schools with social norms marketing programs. In fact, increases in monthly alcohol use and in total volume consumed were observed at some schools. Thus, the creation of social norms programs, while in theory, can reduce underage drinking, there remain a number of questions regarding its actual impact.

Micro-Level Efforts

Detection of Fake IDs

Using fake IDs to obtain alcohol from retailers or at bars and restaurants is widespread, in part because of the relative ease in forging or counterfeiting these documents. In addition, underage drinkers often present merchants, bartenders, and door staff with out-of-state IDs, making validation difficult to determine. Many states have changed their driver's licenses and ID cards to make them more tamper-resistant. For example, some states use a profile photograph of minors to clearly indicate that they are under 21. Others boldly print "Under 21 Until ..." on the face of ID cards. Holograms or indicators that can be seen only under an ultraviolet light can also deter counterfeiting.

Beverage Service Training Programs

The COPS report contends that business owners and managers should set clear policies for their employees regarding checking ID with an eye towards denying service to underage customers. Many states' ABC boards provide free beverage-service-and-sales training to inform participants about state and local ordinances concerning alcohol sales to minors and about penalties for breaking the law.

Minimum-Age Purchase Laws

The primary means to enforce minimum-age purchase laws is to conduct compliance checks of businesses that sell alcohol either on or off premises. Compliance checks typically use underage volunteers who try to gain entry and alcohol service at bars or restaurants or buy alcohol at stores. The volunteer is directed to be truthful about his or her age, if asked, and to present legitimate ID. If the volunteer is able to buy alcohol, the server and manager are cited for violating the minimum-age purchase law.

One of the main ways that young people obtain alcohol from commercial sources is to ask strangers to buy it for them. In "shoulder tap" operations, an undercover operative approaches an adult outside a store and asks the adult to buy him or her alcohol. If the adult agrees and does so, he or she is cited for furnishing alcohol to a minor. Very few of these operations have been evaluated, but case studies suggest that highly publicized operations are likely to have a deterrent effect and reduce the amount of alcohol minors obtain from adults.

Checking IDs

Because there are establishments that will turn a blind eye toward underage drinking in favor of making additional sales, ID checks are a necessary part of a community's overall strategy to minimize underage drinking. Plainclothes or uniformed police officers enter an establishment and check the IDs of everyone drinking alcohol. These ID checks encourage doormen and bartenders to be diligent in their efforts to verify customer age and they show customers that the police support the establishment's policies and procedures.

Social Host Liability

Social host liability refers to the imposition of civil penalties against adults who provide alcohol to minors for injuries caused by them. Approximately 30 states have some form of social-host-liability law. At a minimum, education efforts should stress awareness of relevant laws, penalties, and enforcement initiatives. This type of training has proved particularly effective with fraternities and sororities on college campuses, which have resulted in changes in policy regarding large house parties.

Police have also noted that it is often difficult to identify the adult responsible for providing alcohol to minors at large house parties, particularly keg parties. Keg registration links buyer information to the keg itself, through tags, stickers, or ID numbers stenciled on the keg. At the retail outlet, the buyer must provide ID and contact information, and may also be required to sign a statement indicating awareness that it is illegal to furnish alcohol to minors. When police seize a keg of beer at a party where underage drinking is occurring, the person responsible for furnishing the alcohol can be easily identified through the retailer.

Another innovative strategy for reducing the number of underage drinkers at a party is to issue a summons to the responsible adult for each underage guest found drinking at a party, instead of a single blanket summons for the violation. Typically, the cost of a summons for serving minors is deemed to be a small price to pay compared to the revenue generated from admission fees. This is especially true at college parties. However, if summonses are issued for each offender rather than each offense, the financial implications become more difficult to justify. In fact, it may even encourage alcohol-free events. As Johnson (2004) notes, one jurisdiction issued 70 summonses at one event, resulting in a fine of over $20,000 to the host.

Landlord-Tenant Ordinances and Nuisance Abatement Procedures

Another tactic that can be used to curb underage drinking at parties is to make use of nuisance abatement ordinances or to solicit the assistance of the landlord. When the police are called because of complaints, loud noise, or other disruptive behavior by neighbors, the responding officers can take advantage of existing ordinances to elicit the cooperation of the party's host. Instead of simply issuing a summons, the officers may be able to use local ordinances to threaten eviction if the host does not comply. In all likelihood these ordinances dictate the issuing of a summons for the first offense. However, subsequent citations can lead to other more restrictive plans of action, including eviction if the problem continues.

Suspension of Driver's Licenses

It should be noted that severe criminal penalties for underage drinking-related offenses (e.g., possession, attempted purchase, use of fake ID) are seldom enforced and have not shown to be a significant deterrent. Part of the reason is the priority placed on this activity as well as the costs involved in prosecuting offenders. Recently, several states have attempted a non-criminal sanction to reduce underage drinking. Similar to what is used for those who are truant, offenders have had their driver's licenses suspended for a period of time if they are caught with alcohol, even if the offense does not involve a vehicle. Preliminary evidence has indicated that this may be a promising strategy for underage drinkers (Walsky 2001).

Summary

While most people do not consider underage drinking a serious offense, according to recent figures, about 11 million persons aged 12 to 20 reported drinking alcohol in the past month and about 7 million were binge drinkers. Males are slightly more likely than females to be underage drinkers and are also more likely to binge drink. Whites have highest rates of underage drinking while Asian Americans are least likely to drink. According to the National Center on Substance Abuse at Columbia University, alcohol is the biggest drug problem among children and young adults in this country. Moreover, students are more likely to be affected by alcohol far more extensively than any other type of drug. Nearly 81% of high school students have tried alcohol. This is contrasted with 47% who have used marijuana and 29% who have used another illegal drug.

The alcohol industry spends billions of dollars each year on advertising, which includes sponsorship of events, Internet advertising, and product placements in movies and TV shows (Scheir et al. 2000). Image advertising, which markets an image rather than the quality of a product, is aggressively used by the alcohol industry. Several studies suggest that animation and rock music commonly used in beer advertising campaigns have wide appeal among children and young teens. Children are more familiar with the Budweiser characters than with virtually any other animated figure, including such high profile characters as Smokey the Bear, the Mighty Morphin' Power Rangers, and Kellogg's Frosted Flakes' Tony the Tiger. The implication of this is that the more they identify with the character, the more likely they will choose to drink (Hill et al. 2000).

Relatively recent additions to the product line of the alcohol beverage industry is a new breed of sweet-tasting alcoholic beverages, known as "malternatives" or "alcopops" (e.g., Mike's Hard Lemonade, Tequiza, Smirnoff Ice, Skyy Blue). These beverages are sweet, fruit-flavored, malt-based drinks that come in colorful, child-oriented packaging. Most alcopop beverages have approximately five to seven percent alcohol by volume, a level that is comparable to beer (Alcohol Foundation 2004; Menkengas et al. 1998).

The problems stemming from underage drinking include issues surrounding academic achievement, sexual behavior, including pregnancy, auto accidents, suicide and physical health problems. One of the most significant factors that decrease the risks of underage drinking relates to the relationship the teen has with his or her parents: those with good or excellent relationships are much less likely to start drinking or to continue doing it later in life. There are also a variety of strategies that communities can employ to minimize the effects of underage drinking such as changes to underage drinking laws, raising teens' awareness about drinking, social host laws, beverage service training programs, shoulder tap operations by law enforcement, and suspending the driver's license of any teen caught drinking. In sum, underage drinking is one of the most pervasive problems in American society and despite repeated efforts to curb its effects, it remains one of the most dominant problems facing teenagers in the U.S.

References

Alcohol Foundation. 2001. *"Alcopops" and Kids*. Chapel Hill, NC: Alcohol Foundation.

Baer, J. S. 2002. "Student Factors: Understanding Individual Variation in College Drinking." *Journal of Studies on Alcohol*, 14:40–53.

Biederman, J., Faraone, S. V., Monuteaux, M. C., & Feighner, J. A. 2000. "Patterns of Alcohol and Drug Use in Adolescents can be Predicted by Parental Substance use Disorders." *Pediatrics*, 106(4), 792–797.

Brown, S. A. and D'Amico, E. J. 2001. "Outcomes of Alcohol Treatment for adolescents." in Galanter, M. (ed.) *Research Developments in Alcoholism, Vol. 15: Services Research in the Era of Managed Care*. New York Kluer Academic/Plenum, pp. 307–327.

Brown, S. A., Tapert, S. F., Granholm, E., & Delis, D. C. 2000. "Neurocognitive Functioning of Adolescents: Effects of Protracted Alcohol Use." *Alcoholism: Clinical and Experimental Research*, 24(2), 164–171.

Brown, S. A., Tate, S. R., Vik, P. W., Haas, A. L., & Aarons, G. A. 1999. "Modeling of Alcohol Use Mediates the Effect of Family History of Alcoholism on Adolescent Alcohol Expectancies."*Experimental and Clinical Psychopharmacology*, 7(1), 20–27.

Centers for Disease Control and Prevention. 2000a. *Fact sheet: Youth Risk Behavior Trends from CDC's 1991, 1993, 1995, 1997, and 1999 Youth Risk Behavior*

Surveys. Atlanta, GA: U.S. Department of Health and Human Services, Centers for Disease Control and Prevention.

Centers for Disease Control and Prevention. 2000b. "Youth Risk Behavior Surveillance, United States, 1999." *Morbidity and Mortality Weekly Report* (MMWR), 49(SS05).

Centers for Disease Control and Prevention. 2001. *Suicide in the United States.*

Chesson, H., Harrison, P., & Kassler, W. J. 2000. "Sex Under the Influence: The Effect of Alcohol Policy on Sexually Transmitted Disease Rates in the United States." *Journal of Law and Economics*, 43, 215–238.

Dansky, B. S., Brewerton, T. D., & Kilpatrick, D. G. 2000. "Comorbidity of Bulimia Nervosa and Alcohol Use Disorders: Results from the National Women's Study." *International Journal of Eating Disorders*, 27(2), 180–190.

Dawson, D.A. 2000. "The Link Between Family History and Early Onset Alcoholism: Earlier Initiation of Drinking or More Rapid Development of Dependence?" *Journal of studies on Alcoholism* 61(5): 637–646.

Deas, D., and Thomas, S.E. 2002. "Comorbid Psychiatric Factors Contributing to Adolescent Alcohol and Other Drug Use." *Alcohol Research & Health* 26(2):116–121.

DeWit, D. J., Adlaf, E. M., Offord, D. R., & Ogborne, A. C. 2000. "Age at First Alcohol Use: A Risk Factor for the Development of Alcohol Disorders." *American Journal of Psychiatry*, 157(5), 745–750.

Fletcher, A. C., & Jeffries, B. C. 1999. "Parental Mediators of Associations Between Perceived Authoritative Parenting and Early Adolescent Substance Use." *Journal of Early Adolescence,* 19(4), 465–487.

Fletcher, L. A., Toomey, T. L., Wagenaar, A. C., Short, B., & Willenbring, M. L. 2000. "Alcohol Home Delivery Services: A Source of Alcohol for Underage Drinkers." *Journal of Studies on Alcohol,* 61(1), 81–84.

Grant, B.F., and Dawson, D.A. 1997. "Age of Onset of Alcohol Use and its Association with DSM-IV Alcohol Abuse and Dependence: Results from the National Longitudinal Alcohol Epidemiologic Survey." *Journal of Substance Abuse* 9:103–110.

Greenblatt, J. C. 2000. *Patterns of Alcohol Use among Adolescents and Associations with Emotional and Behavioral Problems.* Rockville, MD: Substance Abuse and Mental Health Services Administration.

Greenfield, T. K. 1998. *Summary of Public Opinion Survey on Alcohol.* Berkley, CA: Public Health Institute.

Greening, L., & Stoppelbein, L. 2000. "Young Drivers' Health Attitudes and Intentions to Drink and Drive." *Journal of Adolescent Health,* 27(2), 94–101.

Grossman, M., Sindelar, J. L., Mullahy, J., & Anderson, R. 1993. "Policy watch: Alcohol and Cigarette Taxes." *Journal of Economic Perspectives,* 7(4), 211–222.

Grover, P. K. 1999. *Preventing Problems Related to Alcohol Availability: Environmental Approaches.* Rockville, MD: U.S. Department of Health and Human Services, Substance Abuse and Mental Health Services Administration, Center for Substance Abuse Prevention.

Grube, J. W. 1993. "Alcohol Portrayals and Alcohol Advertising on Television." *Alcohol Health and Research World,* 17(1), 54–60.

Grube, J. W. 1997. "Preventing Sales of Alcohol to Minors: Results from a Community Trial." *Addiction,* 92(Supplement 2), S251–S260.

Grube, J. W., & Wallack, L. 1994. "Television Beer Advertising and Drinking Knowledge, Beliefs, and Intentions Among Schoolchildren." *American Journal of Public Health,* 84(2), 254–259.

Hill, S. Y., Shen, S., Lowers, L., & Locke, J. 2000. "Factors Predicting the Onset of Adolescent Drinking in Families at High Risk for Developing Alcoholism." *Biological Psychiatry*, 48(4), 265–275.

Johnson, H. L., & Johnson, P. B. 1997. "Understanding Early Adolescent Smoking and Drinking," In B. Bain, H. Janzen, J. Paterson, L. Stewin, & A. Yu (eds.), *Psychology and education in the 21st century—Proceedings of the International Council of Psychologists Convention* (pp. 153–158). Edmonton, Alberta: IC Press.

Kluger, J. 2001. "How to Manage Teen Drinking (the smart way)." *Time*, 157, 42–44.

Komro, K. A. and Toomey, T. L. 2002. "Strategies to Prevent Underage Drinking." *Alcohol Research and Health* 26(1):5–14.

Merikangas, K. R., Stolar, M., Stevens, D. E., Goulet, J., Preisig, M. A., Fenton, B. 1998. "Familial Transmission of Substance Use Disorders." *Archives of General Psychiatry*, 55(11), 973–979.

National Center for Health Statistics. 1998. *Ten Leading Causes of Death, United States: 1998.*

National Highway Traffic Safety Administration. 2000. *Traffic Safety Facts 2000: Alcohol.* Washington, DC: U.S. Department of Transportation.

National Institute on Alcohol Abuse and Alcoholism. 2000. *10th special report to Congress on Alcohol and Health: Highlights from Current Research.* Rockville, MD: U.S. Department of Health and Human Services, National Institute on Alcohol Abuse and Alcoholism.

National Institute on Alcohol Abuse and Alcoholism. 2000. *Make a Difference: Talk to Your Child About Alcohol.* Rockville, MD: U.S. Department of Health and Human Services, National Institute of Alcohol Abuse and Alcoholism.

Pacific Institute for Research and Evaluation. 2003. *Alcohol Beverage Control Enforcement: A Legal Research Report.* Calverton, MD: Pacific Institute for Research and Evaluation.

Pacific Institute for Research and Evaluation, Levy, D. T., Miller, T. R., & Cox, K. 1999. *Costs of Underage Drinking.* Calverton, MD: Pacific Institute for Research and Evaluation.

Mosher, J. F., & Stewart, K. 1999. *Regulatory Strategies for Preventing Youth Access to Alcohol: Best practices.* Calverton, MD: Pacific Institute for Research and Evaluation.

Pacific Institute for Research and Evaluation, & Stewart, K. 1999. *Strategies to Reduce Underage Alcohol Use: Typology and Brief Overview.* Calverton, MD: Pacific Institute for Research and Evaluation.

Richter, L., & Richter, D. M. 2001. "Exposure to Parental Tobacco and Alcohol use: Effects on Children's Health and Development." *American Journal of Orthopsychiatry,* 71(2), 182–203.

Rohde, P., Lewinsohn, P. M., Kahler, C. W., Seeley, J. R., & Brown, R. A. 2001. "Natural Course of Alcohol Use Disorders from Adolescence to Young Adulthood." *Journal of the American Academy of Child and Adolescent Psychiatry,* 40(1), 83–90.

Rose, R. J. 1998. "A Developmental Behavior-Genetic Perspective on Alcoholism Risk." *Alcohol Health and Research World* 22(2): 131–143.

Scheir, L. M., Botvin, G. J., Griffin, K. W., & Diaz, T. 2000. "Dynamic Growth Models of Self-Esteem and Adolescent Alcohol Use." *Journal of Early Adolescence,* 20(2), 178–209.

Spear, L. 2002. "Adolescent Brain and the College Drinker: Biological Basis of Propensity to Use and Misuse alcohol." *Journal of Studies on Alcohol* (Suppl. 14):71–81.

The National Center on Addiction and Substance Abuse (CASA) at Columbia University. 2001. *National Survey of American Attitudes on Substance Abuse VI: Teens.* New York: National Center on Addiction and Substance Abuse (CASA) at Columbia University.

The National Center on Addiction and Substance Abuse (CASA) at Columbia University. 2002. *CASA analysis of Substance Abuse and Mental Health Services Administration.* (1998). National Household Survey on Drug Abuse, 1997 [Data file]. Washington, DC: U.S. Department of Health and Human Services, Substance Abuse and Mental Health Services Administration.

The National Center on Addiction and Substance Abuse (CASA) at Columbia University. 2002. *The economic value of underage drinking and adult excessive drinking to the alcohol industry.* New York: National Center on Addiction and Substance Abuse (CASA) at Columbia University.

Walski, D. 2002. "Drinking on College Campuses." *Campus Law Enforcement Journal* 32(6):20–22.

Wechsler, H., Kuo, M., Lee, H., & Dowdall, G. W. 2000. "Environmental Correlates of Underage Alcohol Use and Related Problems of College Students." *American Journal of Preventive Medicine,* 19(1), 24–29.

Wills, T. A., Vacarro, D., & McNamara, G. 1992. "Role of Life Events, Family Support, and Competence in Adolescent Substance Use: A Test of Vulnerability and Protective Factors." *American Journal of Community Psychology,* 20(3), 349–374.

Wuethrich, B. 2001. "Getting Stupid." *Discover,* 22(3), 57–63.

6

Teen Smoking

Teen smoking is considered a status offense even though it is not noted in the Uniform Crime Reports or the Juvenile Court Statistics. However the lack of attention by delinquency experts should not minimize its significance. In fact, teen smoking is not only considered one of the most preventable of all diseases, affecting millions of teenagers each year, it has linkages to other forms of status offending and delinquency. The use of tobacco products, which includes cigarettes, cigars, and forms of smokeless tobacco products, such as "chew" and "snuff," cause a host of problems for parents, teens, and the general public. In fact, the use of tobacco, specifically smoking, has links to alcohol abuse and other forms of illicit drug abuse. But what can policymakers and parents do about reducing teen smoking? Have any programs worked? Perhaps more importantly, does the effort to reduce smoking, which is not simply confined to teenagers, lead the public to trample over the freedom of choice? This chapter will attempt to address the issues surrounding teen use of tobacco as well as how to minimize its effects.

Evidence of Underage Smoking

Perhaps the two most comprehensive measures of teen smoking come from the 2005 National Drug Use and Health Survey (NDUHS) and the 2005 Monitoring the Future Study (MFS). According to the MFS, the statistics for the use of cigarettes and alcohol, considered licit drugs, are alarming. According to the survey, nearly half of American youth have tried cigarettes by the 12th grade and nearly a quarter of 12th graders are current smokers. An equal number of 8th graders have tried cigarettes and about 10% of that population are considered current smokers. While some experts expressed a level of optimism concerning the decline in cigarette use in the 1990s, by 2006, rates were even higher than before the decline. This is true not only of the use of cigarettes but also attitudes about them. Many changes about cigarettes and smoking in the early 1990s were attributed to the reduction in cigarette advertising as well as anti-smoking campaigns funded by tobacco companies as part of their overall legal settlement. Further, the cost of cigarettes, which rose substantially during this period, was also seen as a deterrent among teens (these costs were designed in part to offset the expenses associated with the tobacco settlement as well as a source of revenue for states in the form of increased excise taxes).

Another area of concern is smokeless tobacco, which comes in two forms. "Snuff" is finely ground tobacco usually sold in tins, either loose or in packets. It is held in the mouth between the lip or cheek and the gums. "Chew" is a leafy form of tobacco, usually sold in pouches. It is held in the mouth and can be chewed. Smokeless tobacco is also sometimes called "spit" tobacco because users spit out the tobacco juices and saliva stimulated by the tobacco that accumulates in the mouth (MFS 2006). While this represents a much smaller segment of the tobacco using teen population, the changes in use, disapproval, and availability, are similar to cigarettes.

According to NDUHS, in 2005 an estimated 71.5 million Americans aged 12 or older were current users of a tobacco product (as defined as using within the past thirty days). This represents about 30% of the population in that age category. About one fourth of tobacco users in 2005 were cigarette smokers, about 6% smoked cigars, 3% used smokeless tobacco and about 1% smoked a pipe. The NDUHS report also indicated that the rates of current users were unchanged from 2004, although there was a slight decrease between 2002 and 2005. Among underage smokers, those between the ages of 12 and 17, there were 3.3 million users of tobacco products in 2005, of which 2.7 million used cigarettes. The rate of past month cigarette use among this segment of the population declined about 2% from 2002. Similar decreases were seen with cigar use while smokeless tobacco use rates remained about the same since 2002. In 2005, 2.4% of 12 or 13 year olds, 9.2% of 14 or 15 year olds, and 20.6% of 16 or 17

Table 6-1
Percentage Use of Tobacco Products by Gender

	Males	Females
Cigarettes	27.4%	22.5%
Cigars	9.6%	1.8%
Smokeless	6.1%	0.4%

Source: National Drug Use Health Survey 2005

year olds were current cigarette smokers. Clearly cigarettes are the preferred tobacco product among underage youth. Smokeless tobacco rates were only about 2% for the 12–17 age group, whereas it was about 5% for those 18–25 years old.

As Table 6-1 shows, in 2005, use of a tobacco product among those aged 12 or older, was higher for males (about 27%) than females (23%). Males clearly dominated past month use for every tobacco product. For example, cigarette smoking was higher among males (27.4% vs. 22.5% of females); cigar smoking (9.6% for males vs. 1.8% of females) and smokeless tobacco (6.1% for males vs. 0.4% of females). However, among youths aged 12 to 17, current cigarette use was about the same for males and females (10.8% vs. 10.7%) The rate of use for females in this age group saw some fluctuation since 2002, with a high of 13.6% in 2002 to a low of 10.8% in 2005. The rate for females during this time period was about 12.3%. For males in this age group, there has been a steady decline since 2002 from 12.3% to 10.7% in 2005.

With regard to race and ethnicity, as Table 6-2 shows, among youths aged 12 to 17, cigarette smoking was more common among Whites than African Americans (31.0% vs. 28.4%). The NDUHS reported that there were not statistically significant changes in past month use between 2004 and 2005 among any race or ethnic group. Interestingly there has been a significant increase in the use of smokeless tobacco among American Indians or Alaska Native: from 3.6% in 2004 to 8.6% in 2005, however no explanation for this increase is offered. What is noted is that the use of smokeless tobacco among all other groups remained the same during that time period.

Table 6-2
Past 30 Day Tobacco Use by Ethnicity

Race/Ethnicity	Percentage
Whites	31.0%
African Americans	28.4%
Hispanic/Latino	24.5%
Asian American	14.6%
Hawaiian/ Pacific Islander	30.3%

Source: National Drug Use Health Survey 2005

As Table 6-3 shows, cigarette use also tends to be related to education levels. Those with more education tend to smoke less. Among adults 18 or older, current cigarette use in 2005 was reported by about 35% of those who had not completed high school and about 14% of college graduates. Interestingly, the use of smokeless tobacco was similar across education levels until the category of college graduates, where it was lower than all other groups. For those who were 18 or older who had not completed high school, the use of smokeless tobacco in the past month was about 3.5%. Only 1.9% of college graduates used smokeless tobacco. One explanation from these findings, might be that as people become more educated they tend to understand the risks associated with smoking.

Table 6-3
Percentage of Cigarette Use and Education Levels

Education Level	Percentage
Less than H.S.	35%
H.S. graduate	32%
Some College	28%
College graduate	14%

Source: National Drug Use Health Survey 2005

Given the costs of cigarettes, particularly in light of high excise taxes, with some packs of cigarettes costing four dollars or more, it would seem that tobacco use and employment would be related. In 2005, current cigarette smoking was more common among the unemployed adults aged 18 or older than among adults who were working full-time or part-time (43.8% for unemployed workers vs. 28.3% full-time and 25.2% of part-time workers). Cigar smoking followed a similar pattern with about 10% of unemployed adults reporting past month use compared to 6.8% of full-time and 5.6% of part-time workers. While it is interesting to note that cigarette use among the unemployed decreased between 2002 and 2005, among full-time workers, current use of smokeless tobacco increased slightly (from 3.7% to 4.2%). This runs counter to most of the research on the relationship between education and tobacco use, and while the change is minor, it is worth noting.

The Connection of Tobacco Use and Other Drugs

According to both the National Drug Use and Health Survey (2005) as well as the Monitoring the Future (2005) reports, the use of illicit drugs and alcohol was more common among current cigarette smokers than nonsmokers. That is, people who smoke also tend to take other drugs, rendering cigarette smoking a gateway activity to different forms of drug abuse. In fact, cigarette smokers are five times more likely to use illicit drugs compared to non-smokers (20.2% vs. 4.1%). Alcohol abuse is also more common among smokers compared to non-smokers. Alcohol use was reported by over two-thirds of current cigarette smokers compared with less than half of those who did not smoke cigarettes (67.6% vs. 46.6%). This connection also relates to binge drinking, where cigarette smokers are approximately three times more likely to binge drink than non smokers (43.8% vs. 15.7%). Heavy drinking is most noted among smokers, who are five times more likely to be heavy drinkers than those who do not smoke (16.1% vs. 3.5%).

It also seems that cigarette smoking is connected to using other tobacco products as well. While only about 5% of cigarette smokers used smokeless tobacco, they are still about twice as likely to use smokeless tobacco than nonsmokers (5% vs. 2.6%). Additionally, cigarette smokers were about four times more likely to smoke cigars than those who did not smoke cigarettes (12.6% vs. 3.3%). Clearly the addictive properties associated with smoking cigarettes makes it much more likely for a user to resort to other forms of tobacco as well (National Drug Use and Health Survey 2005; Monitoring the Future 2005).

The Composition of a Cigarette

So what is in a cigarette that makes it so addictive? What are the contents that make it so dangerous for people to use? According to Action on Smoking and Health, an advocacy group designed to educate people on the risks of smoking, the problem with cigarette smoking has to do with three main elements: tar, nicotine, and carbon monoxide. While some of these are bad enough for a person by themselves, when they are burned and combined with other chemicals, the results are particularly problematic.

The basic elements of a cigarette are the tobacco, the paper, and a filter, if the particular brand has one attached. Essentially, cigarettes are designed to deliver a steady dose of nicotine. The tobacco, which is blended from two main leaf varieties: "Virginia" which contains 2–3% nicotine; and "'Burley" tobacco which has a higher nicotine content (3–4%). Cigarettes sold in the United States also contain up to 10% of imported "Oriental" tobacco which is aromatic but relatively low (less than 2%) in nicotine (Action on Smoking and Health 2006).

In addition to the leaf blend, cigarettes contain fillers, which are made from the stems and other bits of tobacco which would otherwise be waste products. These are mixed with water and various flavorings and additives. The ratio of filler varies among brands. Additives and flavorings are used to preserve tobacco products or to make them smell and taste better. While some of these may appear to be quite harmless in their natural form they may be harmful in combination with other substances. Also, when additives are burned, new products are formed which can be toxic. The nicotine and tar delivery can also be modified by the type of paper used in the cigarette (Action on Smoking and Health 2006).

Filters are made of cellulose acetate and trap some of the tar and smoke particles from the inhaled smoke. Filters also cool the smoke slightly, making it easier to inhale. They were added to cigarettes in the 1950s, in response to the first reports that smoking was hazardous to people's health. Tobacco companies claimed that their filtered brands had lower tar than others and encouraged consumers to believe that they were safer (Action on Smoking and Health 2006). Obviously the real problems associated with cigarettes come when they are smoked. Tobacco smoke contains thousands of different chemicals which are released into the air as particles and gases. Many toxins are present in higher concentrations The smoke includes nicotine, "tar" (itself composed of many chemicals), benzene and benzo(a)pyrene. The gas phase includes carbon monoxide, ammonia, dimethylnitrosamine, formaldehyde, hydrogen cyanide and acrolein. Nearly 60 of these chemicals, including benzo(a)pyrene and dimethylnitrosamine, have been shown to cause cancer (Action on Smoking and Health 2006). "Tar", also known as "total particulate matter," is inhaled when the smoker draws on a lighted cigarette (Action on Smoking and Health 2006).

In the 1950s tar in tobacco smoke was discovered to be associated with the increased risk of lung cancer. In response, tobacco companies gradually reduced the tar levels in cigarettes. Although there is a small decrease in the risk of lung cancer by using lower tar cigarettes, research suggests that these benefits are negated by the tendency of smokers to smoke more of them or to inhale more deeply. Also, a study by the American Cancer Society found that the use of filtered, lower tar cigarettes may be the cause of adenocarcinoma, a particular kind of lung cancer (American Cancer Society 2006).

Nicotine is an extremely powerful drug. Nicotine is contained in the moisture of the tobacco leaf: when the cigarette is lit, it evaporates, attaching itself to the tobacco smoke inhaled by the smoker. It is absorbed by the body very quickly, reaching the brain within seconds. It stimulates the central nervous system, increasing the heart rate and blood pressure, leading to the heart needing more oxygen. Carbon monoxide, the main poisonous gas in car exhausts, is present in all cigarette smoke. It binds to hemoglobin much more readily than oxygen, thus allowing the blood to carry less oxygen (Action on Smoking and Health 2006).

The Effects of Smoking

Cigarette smoking during childhood and adolescence produces significant health problems among young people, including an increase in the number and severity of respiratory illnesses, decreased physical fitness, and potential reduction in the rate of lung growth and the level of maximum lung function. An estimated 440,000 Americans die each year from diseases caused by smoking (American Heart Association 2006).

Each day, nearly 6,000 children under 18 years of age start smoking; of these, nearly 2,000 will become regular smokers—almost 800,000 annually. Approximately 90% of smokers begin smoking before the age of 21. Adolescents who smoke regularly can have just as hard a time quitting as long-time smokers. Of adolescents who have smoked at least 100 cigarettes in their lifetime, most of them report that they would like to quit, but are not able to do so (American Heart Association 2006).

Every time a person smokes a cigarette a number of harmful effects are set in motion. The adrenal glands are stimulated by nicotine causing a release of cortisol and adrenaline. Stored glucose is released by the liver into the bloodstream to provide fast fuel to the muscles. If the fuel is not used, it is stored as fat. Nicotine prevents lipids from metabolizing properly so low-density lipoproteins (LDL) or "bad" cholesterol is increased and High-density lipoproteins (HDL) or "good" cholesterol is reduced (American Heart Association 2006).

Nicotine causes arterial blood vessels to become clogged and blood cannot flow through them properly. Nicotine also constricts blood vessels causing the heart rate, blood pressure, and blood flow to increase. This requires the heart to work harder. Carbon monoxide from the cigarettes takes the place of oxygen in the blood. This means the tissues including the heart and the brain are not getting the oxygen they need. Carbon monoxide also makes it easier for bad cholesterol to get into the blood vessels (American Heart Association 2006).

Long-Term Effects

According to the MFS study, the greatest preventable cause of disease and mortality in the United States is cigarette smoking. According to the American Heart Association, repeated warnings have alerted us to the risks of lung cancer and heart disease associated smoking and exposure to second hand tobacco smoke.

Some argue that heavy use of cigarette smoking is problematic but those who only smoke occasionally are not nearly as at risk as heavy smokers. However, in a new study published in a 2006 issue of the *Journal of Epidemiology and Public Health,* Danish researchers found that smoking as few as three to five cigarettes per day substantially increased the risk of heart attack and death. This finding was true for both men and women, but was especially true in women, in whom "light" smoking (those who smoke only a few cigarettes a day) resulted in a 50% higher incidence of both heart attack and death as compared to men (Mei-Chen, Davies, and Kandel 2006).

Previous studies on light smokers also showed that smoking a relatively small number of cigarettes daily was hazardous to one's health, but in these previous studies a cutoff of 10–20 cigarettes per day was used. Mei-Chen, Davies, and Kandel's (2006) study was the first to document that even a very small number of cigarettes per day is a problem. This new study was accomplished by analyzing data from the Copenhagen City Heart Study, in which 14,223 individuals without evidence of heart disease were followed from 1976 to 1998. A relatively large proportion of these people turned out to be smokers. The researchers found that the more cigarettes one smokes per day, the higher the risk. But the risk remains substantial all the way down to three cigarettes per day. What this means is that cigarette smokers who convince themselves that "cutting back" is good enough still leaves them vulnerable (Mei-Chen, Davies, and Kandel 2006).

The Issue of Secondhand Smoke

Secondhand smoke is a byproduct of cigarette, cigar, or pipe smoking. Secondhand smoke occurs when tobacco burns or when smokers exhale, and it is inhaled involuntarily by non-smokers. Secondhand smoke is composed of two types of smoke. The first is called *side stream smoke,* which is the smoke released from the burning end of a cigarette, a cigar, or from tobacco burning in the bowl of a pipe.

The second is called *mainstream smoke,* which is exhaled by a smoker. When nonsmokers are exposed to secondhand smoke, they inhale many of the same cancer-causing chemicals that smokers inhale. According to the U.S. Surgeon General, cigarette smoke contains more than 4,000 chemical compounds, including more than 50 cancer-causing chemicals, and at least 250 chemicals that are either toxic or carcinogenic (U.S. Surgeon General's Office 2004).

Both side stream and mainstream smoke are dangerous to nonsmokers. For example, because side stream smoke is generated at lower temperatures and under different conditions than mainstream smoke, it contains higher concentrations of many of the toxins found in cigarettes. Secondhand smoke has been designated as a known human carcinogen by the U.S. Environmental Protection Agency, the National Toxicology Program, and the International Agency for Research on Cancer. Secondhand smoke also is listed as an occupational carcinogen by the National Institute for Occupational Safety and Health (U.S. Surgeon General's Office 2004).

Former U.S. Surgeon General Richard H. Carmona issued a warning about the dangers of secondhand smoke. In the report, *The Health Consequences of Involuntary Exposure to Tobacco Smoke,* Carmona said there is no risk-free level of exposure to secondhand smoke. His report shows that nonsmokers who are exposed to secondhand smoke increase their risk of developing heart disease by 25–30% and their risk of lung cancer by 20–30%. This is a major public health concern, because nearly half of all nonsmoking Americans are regularly exposed to secondhand smoke. The Surgeon General's report shows that secondhand smoke exposure can cause heart disease and lung cancer in nonsmoking adults and is a known cause of sudden infant death syndrome (SIDS), respiratory problems, ear infections, and asthma attacks in infants and children.

The report shows that even brief exposure to secondhand smoke can cause immediate harm. The only way to protect nonsmokers from the dangerous chemicals in secondhand smoke is to eliminate smoking indoors, because even the most sophisticated ventilation systems cannot completely eliminate secondhand smoke exposure and only smoke-free environments afford full protection. Many U.S. cities and businesses have banned smoking recently, but others have resisted for fear of losing regular customers or appearing to discriminate against smokers (U.S. Surgeon General's Office 2004).

Why Teens Smoke

Some research suggests that parents' smoking plays an important role in whether their children do—one study revealed that adolescents who had parents that smoked were four times more likely to be a smoker than their peers whose parents had never smoked. This same study found that if parents quit smoking while their children were still young, the chances of them becoming a smoker as a teen were dramatically reduced. Other research points to the influence of friends and older siblings as a main factor in their decision to start smoking. Additionally, ad campaigns that portray smoking as glamorous, sexy, sophisticated, or fostering other positive attitudes increased the likelihood of a teen smoking.

There are also other social rewards that come from smoking. For instance smokers provide other smokers with social interaction, companionship and a common bond. In addition to providing opportunities for social interaction, cigarette smoking can provide other social "benefits." For instance, research has proven the fact that nicotine has the ability to suppress feelings, suppress appetite for food, is used as stimulation after sex, and is a good way to relax from troubles and feelings of insecurities.

There is also the tendency for teens to feel as though they are invulnerable to risks (Perloff 1983). Teens often like to feel important by acting in a risky or dangerous manner—smoking allows them to do that. Most teens also like attention. By smoking, which is attractive in part because it is against the rules and evokes a certain response by adults, teens get a lot of attention (Action on Smoking and Health 2006).

Programs to Prevent Teen Smoking

One of the problems with anti-smoking campaigns is that they not only have a poor track record in terms of success, they inevitably involve a political dimension which makes any assessment of their value difficult. A number of critics argue that for over three decades the U.S. has tried to find a solution to the problem of underage smoking. Billions of dollars have been spent and a host of studies have been conducted. From them, numerous programs and approaches have been tried, all with minimal success. As evidence, critics of teen smoking programs point to the fact that smoking rates are nearly as high as they were twenty years ago (Hamilton 2003).

Essentially, there are several themes that describe the anti-smoking efforts of the past thirty years. In the 1990s, attention was given to such tactics as initiating school-based peer programs and anti-tobacco media campaigns. Though each method had its share of proponents, they have not proven to reduce underage tobacco use or illicit drug use in general. School-based programs, particularly those based on peer or social type programs, were very limited and did little to reduce smoking (See Rooney and Murray 1996; van Teijlingen, Friend and Twin 1996).

Another strategy used to curb teen smoking in the 1990s restricted youth access to tobacco products. Many experts felt that a large part of the teen smoking problem came from the easy accessibility of cigarettes. However, enforcing compliance laws by merchants and illegal sales to minors did not change teens' perceptions of the difficulty in access to tobacco products. The Monitoring the Future study found that teens did not think stricter enforcement would change their ability to acquire cigarettes. Nearly 75% of eighth graders and 90% of 10th graders said that cigarettes would be fairly easy or very easy to get if they wanted them.

Part of the problem with underage smoking is that teens who smoke often feel disconnected from larger groups, such as school, students, and teachers. Additionally, health-based warning labels have shown to have little effect on smoking behavior. Part of the answer relates to teens' sense of invulnerability, but another part must be related to the sense of connectedness to adults. Warning labels and school-based programs only work if the person reading them heeds the warning. That only happens when the person respects the messenger, in this case, society.

Thus, there remain a number of challenges to reducing underage smoking. The efforts used are limited because of the perception of teens: some do not heed the message because of the messenger while others who understand the risks associated with smoking do not feel the risks apply to them. This could explain why so many teens disapprove of smoking because they know it is bad for them, but at the same time, believe few if any of these effects will have an impact on *them*.

American Lung Association's Not On Tobacco Program

More recently, other strategies have tried to reduce teen smoking. For instance, the American Lung Association's Not On Tobacco (N-O-T) offers schools and community groups a unique program for helping teens quit. In collaboration with West Virginia University, N-O-T was designed specifically for teens, using a gender-sensitive, 10-session curriculum that includes booster sessions. Teachers, school nurses, counselors and other staff and volunteers trained by the American Lung Association facilitate the sessions in the schools and other community settings.

N-O-T is designed as a voluntary, non-punitive program for teens. An Alternative-to-Suspension program is also included to address student violations of school tobacco policies. Typically, groups are divided by gender and are led by a same-gender facilitator. This allows teens to discuss issues that relate specifically to males or females and to express their own feelings and experiences in an accepting environment. N-O-T incorporates life management skills to help teens deal with stress, decision-making and peer and family relationships. It also addresses healthy lifestyle behaviors such as alcohol or illicit drug use as well as related health issues such as exercise and nutrition.

Preliminary program evaluation shows almost a quarter of student going through N-O-T quit smoking and almost two-thirds reduced the number of cigarettes smoked during weekdays, while three-quarters reduced the number of cigarettes they smoked on weekends. These results were reported directly by the teens and were chemically validated.

Have Media Campaigns Reduced Teen Smoking?

As was mentioned, the rates of tobacco products are increasing despite anti-smoking campaigns, cost increases, and the tobacco industry's refusal to target teens in ad campaigns. But questions remain about whether the industry has been honest about their efforts to reduce teen smoking. While tobacco-makers emphatically deny that they target young people, many of their promotions just happen to appeal to the underage smokers on whom they depend for future business. These efforts seem to be pitched at three levels. First, like the alcohol industry, tobacco manufacturers have begun marketing flavored cigarettes with names such as Kauai Kolada, Twista Lime, and Mandarin Mint, giving curious teens new reasons to try smoking. R.J. Reynolds, which markets the Camel "exotic blends," says they are not aimed at teens. Yet, according to surveys released in May 2004 by the Roswell Park Cancer Institute in Buffalo, about 20% of smokers ages 17 through 19 tried a flavored cigarette, compared with less than 9% of smokers older than 19. At age 55, the interest in flavored products dropped to 2%

Second, also like their alcohol counterparts, the tobacco industry seems to have increased its spending on promotions despite agreeing to curtail or stop certain types of marketing. According to an Federal Trade Commission report in 2003, since signing a deal in 1998 with state officials across the country to curtail certain types of marketing, the industry has more than doubled its expenditures on advertising and promotions. In 2003, major tobacco companies spent $15.1 billion–$22 for every dollar the states spent on tobacco prevention. The bulk of industry spending was on price discounts.

Finally, tobacco companies have also tried to renege on the settlement agreement they signed in the late 1990s. As part of the 1998 settlement, tobacco companies agreed to help fund a national anti-smoking advertising campaign aimed at teens. But in 2002, the Lorillard Tobacco Co. threatened to sue the group running the campaign, claiming it violated the deal by vilifying the tobacco industry. In 2003, a Delaware judge ruled that the advertising campaign did not violate the terms of the tobacco compromise. While the rates of smoking are changing and questions remain about the value of deterrent advertising and price hikes, it is interesting that the industry claims not to target teens but object when teens are given anti-smoking information.

Do Programs Really Work?

In general, a review of the research on smoking cessation programs geared to teen smokers are effective (Sussman et al. 2006). Teens who participate are more likely to kick the tobacco habit than those who attempt to quit on their own. "Most teens who are smokers do want to quit, but they need a lot of help, just as adults do," said Steve Sussman, Ph.D., of the University of Southern California. "The good news is that teen smoking cessation looks promising. Programs have been developed that as a group are showing some effects.

The most effective programs seem to be those that enhance motivation to quit, teach problem-solving skills or other cognitive-behavioral techniques to help teens cope with stress and temptation, or combat social influences that encourage smoking. In the latest issue of *Health Psychology*, a series of articles review the literature on treatment programs for smokers. Each article focused on a specific psychological assessment or treatment conducted in the context of a physical disease process or risk reduction effort.

Programs that used cognitive-behavioral techniques or strategies to enhance motivation had significantly higher rates of success. These two theoretical approaches accounted for two-thirds of the studies included in the review. Social influence programs, which counter tobacco industry promotions, media images and peer pressure, also significantly increased the quit rate. Programs conducted in classrooms or school clinics seemed to be more effective than programs conducted in other settings, such as medical clinics (Sussman et al. 2006).

School-based programs tended to use the most effective theoretical approaches, so it is difficult to determine whether the school setting or the content of the programming was responsible for the greater success of school-based programs. The number of sessions included in a program was also a significant factor in success. Programs that had at least five sessions were more likely to be successful than those with four or fewer sessions. Interestingly, the review found that studies with a follow-up greater than 12 months showed higher quit rates than studies with a shorter follow-up. Among studies of adult smokers, quit rates usually decline with longer follow-up (Sussman et al. 2006).

In a recent Centers for Disease Control survey of high school students, 61% of teen smokers wanted to quit smoking and a similar percentage reported trying to quit during the previous 12 months. According to Robin Mermelstein, Ph.D., director of the Center for Health Behavior Research at the University of Illinois at Chicago, this systematic review provides reason for optimism, but important questions remain unanswered. "There are specific types of programming that we can offer to adolescents and feel confident that what we're offering is better than if they just try on their own," she said. "But overall quit rates for teens are disappointingly low—substantially lower than what we see with adults. We need to start to understand who this works for and why. What are we missing here to boost those rates higher?" (Sussman et al. 2006)

What about Smoker's Rights?

One of the more radical, and, perhaps, largest critics of the approach taken to reduce teen smoking is a group called FOREST, which stands for Freedom Organization for the Right to Enjoy Smoking Tobacco. Created in 1979, FOREST defends the interests of adult smokers. While they object to underage smoking, they eschew the anti-smoking message that teens get, which argues that smokers have a near certainty that they will become afflicted with a smoking-related disease at some point in their lives. In drawing a line between education and propaganda, FOREST believes that the "quit or die" message given to teens, as well as the "data" concerning the effects of smoking, is unreasonable.

Second, the group contends that the second primary tool to reduce underage smoking, by holding retailers responsible for determining the age of the person to whom they sell tobacco products, is untenable. Advocates argue that it is virtually impossible for a store employee to accurately determine whether a person is of sufficient age to purchase tobacco products. This is true even when they present a valid-looking form of identification. FOREST also claims that undercover operations, where authorities set up "sting" operations to catch store owners, amounts to little more than entrapment.

Instead of such unreasonable and punitive measures, which do not address the issue of stopping youth from smoking in the first place, FOREST contends that supervised smoking breaks in public schools would be more reasonable. This is particularly true given that completely banning smoking is unenforceable and results in students finding secret places to smoke on campus which could lead to fire hazards and other safety concerns. FOREST also contends that supervised breaks would likely reduce smoking since few students would want to smoke under supervision. At the same time, however, advocates are quick to point out that smoking is an addiction and has physiological implications that go beyond the willpower of individual smokers.

Finally, advocates are against the policies that excessively tax cigarettes, which increase their overall costs. Citing the problems stemming from the creation of a black market, which meets the demands of the smoker population anyway, this group contends that by reducing the excise tax on tobacco products, especially cigarettes, the safety of the product consumers are buying is assured (See http://www.forest.org).

Summary

By most accounts, teen smoking is one of the most preventable of all diseases and affects millions of teenagers each year. While the U.S. saw dramatic decreases in the use of tobacco by teens in the 1990s, use rates have increased sharply since 2000 and now even exceed previously high levels of use. According to some surveys nearly half of American youth have tired cigarettes by the 12th grade and nearly a quarter of 12th graders are current smokers. An equal number of 8th graders have tried cigarettes and about 10% of that age group are current smokers.

According to the National Drug Use and Health Survey, in 2005, an estimated 71.5 million Americans age 12 or older were current users of tobacco products. Among underage smokers, those between the ages of 12 and 17, there were 3.3. million users of tobacco in 2005, most of them cigarettes. Each day nearly 6,000 children under the age of 18 start smoking, which is almost 800,000 annually. The use rates for tobacco products are higher for males, except for 8th graders, where the rates were nearly identical. Whites were more likely to use cigarettes than any other group and there is a relationship between education and cigarette use. Generally speaking the higher the education level, the less likely a person is to smoke.

Tobacco use is also associated with other forms of drug use. The issue of secondhand smoke is a pervasive one, particularly since certain types of second hand smoke are as dangerous for the non-smoker as the person using cigarettes. Most of the programs designed to curb teen smoking have had only moderate success. Some experts claim that part of the reason has to do with the intensive media campaigns by tobacco companies to undermine anti-smoking efforts. Pro-smoking groups contend that while they do not advocate the use of tobacco by teens, current efforts to reduce underage smoking are unreasonable and counterproductive.

References

Action on Smoking and Health. Fact Sheet #12. November 2006.

Hamilton, W. 2003. "What Shall We Do About the Kids?" *Forces International.*

Department of Health and Human Services, Office of Applied Studies. 2005. *National Drug Abuse and Health Survey.* Washington, D.C.: U.S. Government Printing Office.

Mei-Chen H., Davies, M and Kandel, D.B. 2006. "Epidemiology and Correlates of Daily Smoking and Nicotine Dependence Among Young Adults in the United States." *American Journal of Public Health* 96(2):299–308.

National Institute on Drug Abuse. *Monitoring the Future 2005*. Ann Arbor, MI: University of Michigan.

Perloff, L. 1983. "Perceptions of Vulnerability to Victimization." *Journal of Social Issues*, 39(2):41–61.

Sussman S., Sun P., Dent C.W. 2006. "A Meta-analysis of Teen Cigarette Smoking Cessation." *Health Psychology* 25(5).

7

The Future of Status Offenders and Delinquents

As we have seen, the problems presented by status offenders are serious, considerable, and are not likely to change in the foreseeable future. What is also unlikely to change is the way the juvenile justice system treats status offenses. The debate about whether or not this group of youth should remain under the control of the court system will continue, with no reasonable conclusions being drawn. The sad reality is that many children are likely to fall through the cracks as a result of a punitive philosophy that seems content to punish some offenders simply because they have been born to the wrong families, have grown up in a disadvantaged environment, or have attempted to flee what would otherwise be a dysfunctional situation. Granted, not all status offenders fall into this category, with some committing delinquent acts for which they should be punished. However, questions still remain about the future of status offenders as well as how delinquents will be treated. As changes occur in the justice process for juveniles, with an emphasis on increasingly treating them as adult offenders, inevitably that philosophical shift will impact status offenders. Moreover, given that the problems that create situations where youth runaway from home, skip school, do not obey their parents, or begin abusing drugs and alcohol to cope continue, it is likely that the number of status offenders will increase. This may not be reflected in the statistics, however, since many of these youth will likely find themselves arrested and charged with delinquent acts rather than simply with referrals or treated differently.

At the same time, the question of what to do with youth who consistently disobey their parents, runaway from home, skip school, and use drugs, is difficult to answer. What resources are available for parents who are simply incapable of eliciting the cooperation of their children? Holding them financially and even criminally responsible for the actions of their children does not seem to hold much promise. Additionally, what recourse should society have when a youth is admonished to attend school regularly or to refrain from running away, only to continue to persist even after a judge orders him or her to comply? Short of the threat of incarceration, what avenues can society pursue that evoke the correct behavior? This is particularly true of offenders who not only engage in status offenses, but also partake in other forms of delinquency.

What most experts can agree on are the consequences of such actions. Few dispute the idea that status offenses have particularly negative consequences for society as well as the offender. Truancy serves as a gateway activity for more serious forms of delinquency, running away has an assortment of risks associated with it, underage drinking and smoking represent perhaps the greatest public health risk to teens, while curfew violations can lead to gang activity as well as various forms of victimization. Clearly this is an area of concern, however, as was mentioned in the first chapter, the focus for policymakers appears to be more reactionary; that is, punishing the behavior once it occurs rather than attempting to deal with the causes of the problem.

It seems obvious that the behaviors identified in this book are more symptomatic of larger issues than they are concerns alone. Granted, the behaviors are troubling and can lead to other serious problems, but increasing emphasis seems to be on using punishment as a deterrent to stop the behavior rather than asking what is causing the behavior in the first place. This may be due to an inability to address the causal issues, resulting in a "band-aid" approach. However, this coupled with a more crime control philosophy, ends up placing many youth in greater jeopardy than if society did nothing at all. At least without the stigma of "delinquent" attached to their behavior, some youth might not have a host of negative labels attached to their identity. This is not to say that teens should not be held accountable or that their behavior is ignored. Rather it does point out that fear (of punishment) is a short-term motivator and at some point loses its ability to deter behavior. This leads to an escalation of the severity of punishment, which further alienates children from the very people who are committed to helping them. In the end, it may not mean much to most Americans when we hear children skip school, drink alcohol, smoke, or violate their curfew. However, the consequences for getting caught for such behavior can have a deleterious effect on the teens who are arrested for engaging in such activities. This only drives them further away from the people that might be able to help them.

Selected Bibliography

Adams, K. 2003. "The Effectiveness of Juvenile Curfews at Crime Prevention." *The Annals of the American Academy of Political and Social Science*, 587(1): 136–159.

Aitken, M. 2003. *Community Curfews for Youth: Punitive or Positive?* Ann Arbor, MI: The Search Institute.

ACLU Challenges San Diego's Curfew Law; Lawsuit Filed in Federal Court on Behalf of Teenagers, Parents, Press Release by American Civil Liberties Union, March 15, 1995.

Auerswald, C. L., & Eyre, S. L. 2002. "Youth homelessness in San Francisco: A life cycle approach." *Social Science & Medicine*, 54, 1497–1512.

Baker, M. L., Signmon, J. N., and Nugent, M. E. 2001.*Truancy Reduction: Keeping Students in School*. Washington, D.C.: U.S. Department of Justice, Office of Juvenile Justice Programs, Office of Juvenile Justice and Delinquency Prevention.

Bannister, A. J.; Carter, D.L. and Schafer J. 2001. "A National Police Sure on the Use of Juvenile Curfews." *Journal of Criminal Justice* 29(3):23–240.

Bao, W., Whitbeck, L., & Hyot, D. 2000. "Abuse, support, and depression among homeless and runaway adolescents." *Journal of Health and Social Behavior*, 41, 408–420.

Baron, S. 2003. "Street youth violence and victimization." *Trauma, Violence, & Abuse*, 4(1), 22–44.

Baron, S., & Hartnagel, T. 1998. "Street youth and criminal violence." *Journal of Research in Crime and Delinquency*, 35, 66–192.

Baron, S., Kennedy, L., & Forde, D. 2001. "Male street youths' conflict: The role of background subcultural and situational factors." *Justice Quarterly*, 18, 759–789.

Barry P., Ensign J., & Lipke S. 2002. "Embracing street culture: Fitting health care into the lives of street youth." *Journal of Transcultural Nursing*, 13(2), 145–152.

Bass, D. 1995. "Runaways and homeless youths." *Encyclopedia of Social Work* (19th ed.). Washington, DC: NASW Press.

Bazemore, G.; Stinchcomb, J. B. and Leip, L. A. 2004. "Scared Straight or Bored Straight? Testing Deterrence Logic in an Evaluation of Police-Led Truancy Intervention." *Justice Quarterly* 21(2):269–300.

Bell, A. J., Rosen, L. A. and Dynlacht, D. 1994. "Truancy Intervention." *The Journal of Research and Development in Education*, 27: 203–211.

Berg, I. 1997. "School Refusal and Truancy." *Archives of Disease in Childhood* 76(2):90–92.

Berliner, B. 2002. "Helping homeless students keep up." *Education Digest*, 68(1), 49–52.

Biehal, N., & Wade, J. 2002. "Going missing from residential and foster care: Linking biographies and contexts." *British Journal of Social Work*, 30, 211–225.

Biggar, H. 2001. "Homeless children and education: An evaluation of the Stewart B. McKinney Homeless Assistance Act." *Child and Youth Services Review*, 23(12), 941–969.

Bilchik, S. 1996. *Curfew: An Answer to Juvenile Delinquency and Victimization?* Washington, DC: Office of Juvenile Justice and Delinquency Prevention. Blau, J. 1992. *The Visible Poor*. New York: Oxford University Press.

Booth, R., Zhangb, Y., & Kwiatkowski, C. 1999. "The challenge of changing drug and sex risk behaviors of runaway and homeless adolescents." *Child Abuse and Neglect*, 23(12), 1295–1306.

Brennan, T., Huizinga, D., and Elliott, D. S. 1978. *The Social Psychology of Runaways*. Lexington, MA: Lexington Books.

Brooks, R., Milburn, N., Rotheram-Borus, M., & Witkin, A. 2004. "The system-of-care for homeless youth: Perceptions of service providers." *Evaluation and Program Planning*, 27(4), 443–451.

Bruchey, S. (ed.). 1999. *The Impact of Multiple Childhood Trauma on Homeless and Runaway Adolescents*. New York: Garland Publishing.

Budd, J.1999. *Juvenile Curfews: The Rights of Minors vs. the Rhetoric of Public Safety*. Washington, DC: American Bar Association

Civil Rights Project Harvard University Conference. 2000. *Opportunities Suspended: The Devastating Consequences of Zero Tolerance and School Discipline Policies*.

Craig, T., & Hodson, S. 1998. "Homeless youth in London: Childhood antecedents and psychiatric disorder." *Psychological Medicine*, 28, 1379–1388.

Dalton, M., & Pakenham, K. 2002. "Adjustment of homeless adolescents to a crisis shelter: Application of a stress and coping model." *Journal of Youth and Adolescence*, 31(1), 79–89.

Department of Commerce, U.S. Census Bureau. 2006. Facts for Features. *Oldest Baby Boomers Turn 60*. Washington, DC: U.S. Government Printing Office.

English, A. 1995. "Guidelines for adolescent health research: Legal perspectives." *Journal of Adolescent Health*, 17, 277–286.

Ennett, S., Bailey, S., & Federman, E. 1999. "Social network characteristics associated with risky behaviors among runaway and homeless youth." *Journal of Health and Social Behavior*, 40(1), 63–78.

Ensign, J. 2003. "Ethical issues of qualitative research with homeless youth." *Journal of Advanced Nursing*, 43(1), 43–50.

Ensign, J., & Bell, M. 2004. "Illness experiences of homeless youth." *Qualitative Health Research*, 14(9), 1239–1254.

Eugene, N. 1997. "Street life: Aggravated and sexual assaults among homeless and runaway adolescents." *Youth & Society*, 28(3), 267–290.

Fleisher, M. 1995. *Beggars and Thieves*. Madison: University of Wisconsin Press.

Flowers, R. B. 2001. *Runaway Kids and Teenage Prostitution*. Westport, CT: Praeger.

Ghant, J. 2004. Annotation, *Validity and Construction of Curfew Statute, Ordinance or Proclamation*, 59 A.L.R. 3d 321 (2004).

Greene, J., Ennett, S., & Ringwalt, C. 1999. "Prevalence and correlates of survival sex among runaway and homeless youth." *American Journal of Public Health*, 89(9), 1406–1409.

Greene, J., Ringwalt, C., & Iachan, R. 1997. "Shelters for runaway and homeless youths: Capacity and occupancy." *Child Welfare*, 76, 549–561.

Hagan, J., & McCarthy, B. 1997. *Mean streets: Youth crime and homelessness*. Cambridge, MA: Cambridge University Press.

Halcon, L., & Lifson, A. 2004. "Prevalence and predictors of sexual risks among homeless youth." *Journal of youth and adolescence*, 33(1) 71–80.

Handler, J. F. and Zatz, J. (eds.) 1982. *Neither Angels Nor Thieves: Studies in Deinstitutionalization of Status Offenders*. Washington, DC: National Academy Press.

IT Management. 2006. "Generation X for Dummies." http://www.eweek.com/article.

Johnson, T., Aschkenasy, J., Herbers, M., & Gillenwater, S. 1996. "Self-reported risk factors for AIDS among homeless youth." *AIDS Education and Prevention*, 8, 302–322.

Jones, L. R. 2005. "Ending School Truancy in One Step." *New Jersey Law Journal*, March 7, 2005.

"Juvenile Curfews and the Major Confusion over Minor Rights." *Harvard Law Review*, 2005, vol. 118:2400–2421.

Juvenile Justice Update. 2000. "New Research Fails to Support Effectiveness of Youth Curfew Laws." 6(3): 1, June/July.

Kidd, S., & Scrimenti, K. 2004. "Evaluating child and youth homelessness." *Evaluation Review*, 28(4), 325–341.

Kipke, M., Montgomery, S., Simon, T., Unger, J., & Johnson, T. 1997. "Homeless youth: Drug use patterns and HIV risk profiles according to peer affiliation." *AIDS and Behavior*, 1(4), 247–259.

Klein, J., Woods, A., Wilson, K., Prospero, M., Greene, J., & Ring-walt, C. 2000. "Homeless and runaway youth's access to health care." *Journal of Adolescent Health*, 27, 331–339.

Kurtz, D., Lindsey, E., Jarvis, S., & Nackerud, L. 2000. "How runaway and homeless youth navigate troubled waters: The role of formal and informal helpers." *Child and Adolescent Social Work*, 17(5), 381–402.

Lersch, K. M. and Sellers, C. S. 2000. "A Comparison of Curfew and Noncurfew Violators Using a Self-Report Delinquency Survey." *American Journal of Criminal Justice* 24(2):259–270.

Lindsey, E., & Williams, N. 2002. "How runaway and homeless youth survive adversity: Implications for school social workers and educators." *School Social Work Journal*, 27(1), 1–21.

MacLean, M., Embry, L., & Cauce, A. 1999. "Homeless adolescents' paths to separation from family: Comparison of family characteristics, psychological adjustment, and victimization." *Journal of Community Psychology*, 27(2), 179–187.

Mallett, S., Rosenthal, D., Myers, P., Milvurn, N., & Rotheram-Borus, M. 2003. "Practicing homelessness: A typology approach to young people's daily routines." *Journal of Adolescence*, 27, 337–349.

Markward, M., & Biros, E. 2001. "McKinney revisited: Implications for school social work." *Children and Schools*, 23(3), 182–188.

Maxon, C. and Klein, M. 1997. *Responding to Troubled Youth*. New York: Oxford University Press.

McCluskey, C.P., Bynum, T. S., Patchin, J. W. 2004. "Reducing Chronic Absenteeism: An Assessment of an Early Truancy Initiative." *Crime and Delinquency* 50(2):214.

McDowell, D.; Loftin, C., and Weirsema, B. 2000. "The Effectiveness of Juvenile Curfews on Crime Prevention." *Crime and Delinquency* 46:76–91.

McElvain, J. and Kposowa, A. 2006. "Juvenile Delinquency and Crime Prevention: An Evaluation of a Multi-Agency School Implemented Program." *Journal of California Law Enforcement* 40(4):7–23.

Mogulescu, S. and Segal, H. J. 2002. Approaches to Truancy Prevention. New York: Vera Institute of Justice, Youth Justice Program.

NAS Recruitment Communication. 2006. *Generation Y: The Millennias, Ready or Not,* Here They Come.

National Coalition for the Homeless. 2002. How may people experience homelessness? (NCH Fact Sheet #2). Washington, DC.

Noell, J., Rohde, P., Seeley, J., & Och, L. 2001. "Maltreatment among runaway and homeless youth." *Child Abuse and Neglect,* 25(1), 137–148.

Nunez, R. 1995. *An American family myth: Every child at risk.* New York: Homes for the Homeless.

Pearce, K. 1995. "Street kids need us too: Special characteristics of homeless youth." *Parks & Recreation,* 30(12), 16.

Puzzanchera, C., Stahl, A. L., Finnegan, T. A., Tierney, N., Snyder, H. N. 2003. Juvenile Court Statistics 1998. Washington, D.C.: U.S. Department of Justice, Office of Juvenile Justice and Delinquency Prevention

Snyder, H. N. and Sickmund, M. 1995. *Juvenile Offenders and Victims: A National Report.* Washington, D.C.: U.S. Department of Justice, Office of Juvenile Justice and Delinquency Prevention

Stover, D. 2005. "New Ways, More Reasons to Fight Truancy." *The Education Digest,* 70(5):48–52.

Strickland, V. P. 1998. *Attendance and Grade Point Average: A Study.* East Lansing, MI: National Center for Research on Teacher Learning.

Wright, B., Caspi, A., Moffitt, T., & Silva, P. 1998. "Factors associated with doubled-up housing—A common precursor to homelessness." *Social Service Review,* 72(1), 92–111.

Zemke, R., Raines, C. and Filipczak, B. 2000. *Generations at Work: Managing the Clash of Veterans, Boomers and Xers and Nexters in your Workplace.* New York: American Management Association.

Index